Life At The Extreme

The Volvo Ocean Race Round The World 2005–2006

Rob Mundle

nomad press

Nomad Press
A division of Nomad Communications

10 9 8 7 6 5 4 3 2 1
Copyright ©2006 Volvo Trademark Holding AB

Printed and bound in Singapore

ISBN 0-9771294-8-9

Questions regarding the ordering of this book
should be addressed to:
Nomad Press
2456 Christian St.
White River Junction, VT 05001
www.nomadpress.net
info@nomadpress.net

To the Volvo Ocean Race sailors . . .

Without you there is no adventure, and without your adventure there are no incredible tales on which others living in a cloistered world can thrive

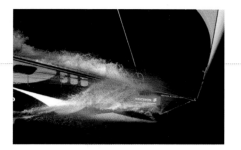

Contents

THE ROUTE | iv

GÖTEBORG
SWEDEN

LEG 8

LEG 9

EUROPE

PORTSMOUTH
ENGLAND

NEW YORK
UNITED STATES

ROTTERDAM
THE NETHERLANDS

LEG 7

NORTH AMERICA

LEG 6

VIGO
SPAIN

BALTIMORE/ANNAPOLIS
UNITED STATES

LEG 5

LEG 1

AFRICA

SOUTH AMERICA

RIO DE JANEIRO
BRAZIL

CAPE TOWN
SOUTH AFRICA

LEG 4

LEG 2

TheRoute

Foreword

In early May, when I was asked to write the foreword for this book, it seemed a straightforward assignment. At the time the skippers had just held their pre-start press conference in Baltimore and were preparing for the 400-mile sprint to New York.

From the sidelines we had watched the adventure of the Volvo Ocean Race unfold. It was a familiar story—the yachts, the competitors, and above all, the racing.

Few people who have had the privilege of racing through the Southern Ocean would not have wished they had been there. The Volvo Open 70 is a superb racing yacht. Day after day we watched 24-hour runs that would have been only a dream in a Volvo Ocean 60. The sustained speeds were astonishing. For the teams and the public following the race from afar, the adventure and drama were back in round-the-world racing.

Then, in the space of a few days, the tragic death of Hans Horrevoets, and then *movistar's* crew taking to the life raft, reminded us that the sport we love can be very dangerous.

Hans' death confirmed that round-the-world racing is an extreme sport. It is a tribute to the professionalism of everyone involved that accidents are few, but the risk will never be eliminated entirely.

The Volvo Ocean Race is a showcase for superb seamanship and teamwork. The next generation of Volvo Open 70s will be stronger, the forces on their structures better understood, and the crews will know more about sailing the yachts hard and safely.

Nothing will ever stop men and women from wanting to race around the world. And it is because of the Volvo Ocean Race 2005–06 that a new generation is waiting for the chance to test themselves against the oceans and be first across the line.

Grant Dalton
Auckland, New Zealand

Raisin

"The sea is immense, precious, and divine, but it is also strong when it wants. We must always respect it and be cautious."
Horacio Carabelli, crewmember, *Brasil 1*

The last 2 days have been extremely difficult aboard *Brasil 1*. The loss on *ABN AMRO TWO* has left us speechless: silence reigns. Everyone knew that the chance of surviving such an accident was small. In moments like this we are thrown back to earth and regain a consciousness of our mortality. We think about our families, our friends, and everything that life gave us and then start to see everything from a different angle.

the Curtain

Horacio Carabelli

Conditions were not easy. The night was dark, the waves were huge, and the wind was blowing at 30 to 40 knots. As soon as Marcel shouted, 'To the rescue' from the nav station we were ready to go: all hands were on deck and prepared for action as we started the long, 60-mile journey to the search area.

We discussed the best way to find someone out there. We sailed for some hours, just slamming and hitting waves. I thought that at one point the boat would simply break in the middle. When we received the news that they had found and recovered the sailor, the crew was relieved, even though we knew that his chance of survival was not great. After race headquarters stood us down from the search we worked on getting back into the race.

We completed some work on deck then decided to set the spinnaker. All the time the crew was anxious for news from *ABN AMRO TWO*. The moment we were told what had happened a feeling of sadness took control of everyone. We were all thinking about Hans and the family he had left.

Aboard *Brasil 1* we were struggling against the sea's huge force. The wind blew more than 30 knots while the waves got higher and higher. We were back to racing mode but soon the boat was almost uncontrollable with the spinnaker up. We were bouncing from one wave to another and nose-diving so deep that the cockpit was always full with water. We gave up on the spinnaker and set a smaller sail. One life already had been lost in this situation.

We sailed the entire night like this. Then, when the sun was up and the wind speed decreased to 27 knots, we decided to raise the spinnaker again. The wind stayed the same for some hours then it went back to between 30 and 35 knots. Controlling the boat was a challenge as it dived into each wave. The pressure on the mast and the sails was enormous and the noise below deck from the water hitting the hull was almost deafening.

In one of these dives there was a massive BANG! The spinnaker pole broke 1 metre from the bow. We reacted fast. Andy Meiklejohn and Stu Wilson ran forward to get the remaining pieces. Luckily the spinnaker was still attached to the boat and we didn't suffer a huge loss of speed. Andy and Stu were still on the bow recovering the biggest piece of the pole—the pole is quite a big tube, 10.5 metres in length and 25 centimetres in diameter—when a wave washed them down the deck. The spinnaker pole was a projectile coming at full speed towards the cockpit. I saw that huge tube and the sharp ends flying centimetres from my face. In a split second I imagined the worst: the tube hitting Torben, who was behind the wheel. We were lucky. Torben ducked and the pole hit the wheel and became stuck between it and the pedestal. Suddenly we didn't have control of the boat! We couldn't steer!

We got the pole out of there and regained control, then, seconds after everything happened, we were just looking at each other in disbelief. We all knew that the consequences of this accident could have been fatal.

Horacio Carabelli
Brasil 1

Putti

This Volvo Ocean Race was to be a challenge encompassing every conceivable element in the ultimate test of sporting prowess, especially when it came to the physical and emotional boundaries of the human body—endurance, athleticism, tactical and technical skills, survival, and sheer guts.

ng "Extreme" into Perspective

The Black Pearl *screams out of Port Phillip Bay, Melbourne, on the way to Wellington.*

50-knot driving rain and gale-force winds off Cape Horn on board Ericsson.

Imagine a sport where the participants put themselves under the same levels of stress as a soldier fighting on the front line in a war!

That's the reality when it comes to the Volvo Ocean Race Round The World—proven by medical research during the previous event.

And, as if that wasn't enough, this time around the fight to be first to finish would be even tougher than those previously contested, setting a considerably higher reference point for extreme sport as we know it. Participants would be pushed even closer to the brink, to that precarious point of balance where one error or an unseen hazard could deliver cataclysmic consequences. It was a threat they would face not just once: it would be ever-present over months of competition, staged in a coliseum comprising the most menacing of oceans. This would be Life at the Extreme—a 31,350-nautical-mile endurance test around the planet under sail.

Amazingly, despite the dangers, the players rolled the dice of life with great conviction. Their attitude was fuelled by an unrelenting spirit of adventure and a determination to survive the most intense weather and wildest seas that Mother Nature could muster, all in the name

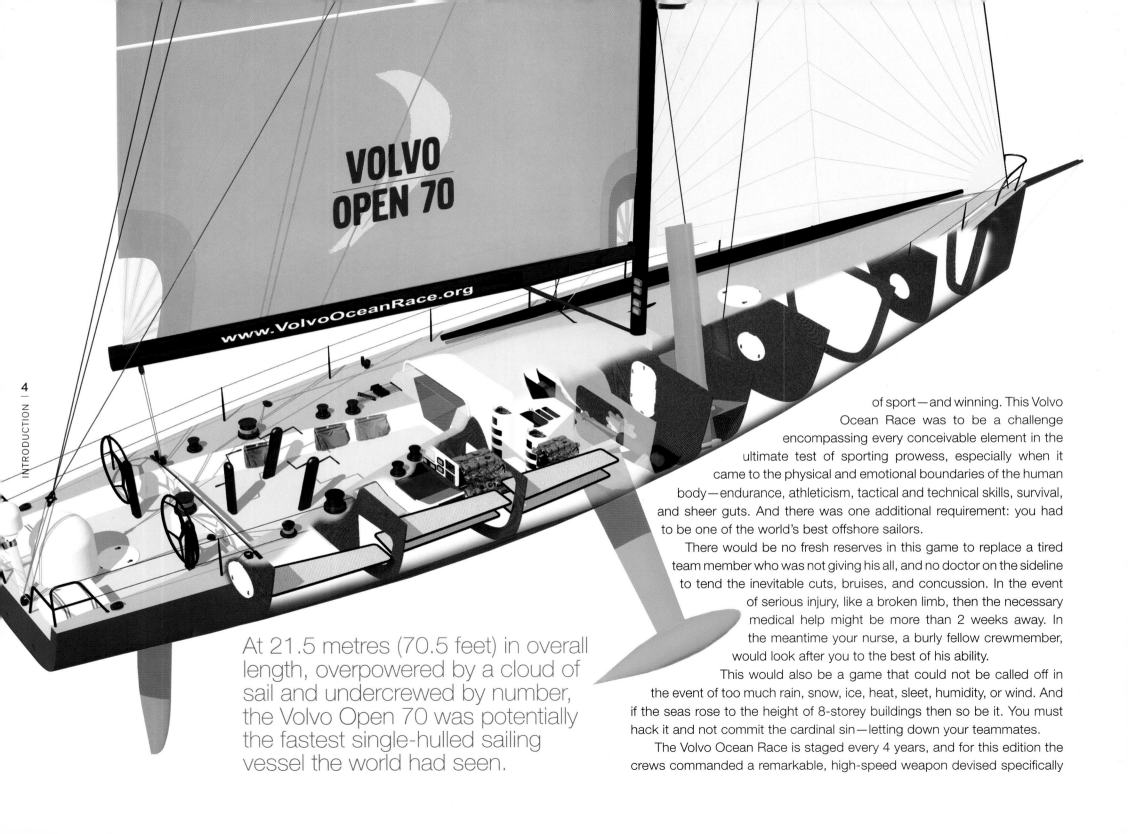

At 21.5 metres (70.5 feet) in overall length, overpowered by a cloud of sail and undercrewed by number, the Volvo Open 70 was potentially the fastest single-hulled sailing vessel the world had seen.

of sport—and winning. This Volvo Ocean Race was to be a challenge encompassing every conceivable element in the ultimate test of sporting prowess, especially when it came to the physical and emotional boundaries of the human body—endurance, athleticism, tactical and technical skills, survival, and sheer guts. And there was one additional requirement: you had to be one of the world's best offshore sailors.

There would be no fresh reserves in this game to replace a tired team member who was not giving his all, and no doctor on the sideline to tend the inevitable cuts, bruises, and concussion. In the event of serious injury, like a broken limb, then the necessary medical help might be more than 2 weeks away. In the meantime your nurse, a burly fellow crewmember, would look after you to the best of his ability.

This would also be a game that could not be called off in the event of too much rain, snow, ice, heat, sleet, humidity, or wind. And if the seas rose to the height of 8-storey buildings then so be it. You must hack it and not commit the cardinal sin—letting down your teammates.

The Volvo Ocean Race is staged every 4 years, and for this edition the crews commanded a remarkable, high-speed weapon devised specifically

Bottom left: The rough hands of Erle Williams, on board The Black Pearl.

Left: Ericsson has a close encounter with movistar during the Melbourne in-port race.

Below: An exhausted Andy Meiklejohn on the grinder on board Brasil 1.

Right: Brunel's bow buries into a wave in big seas.

for the test: the Volvo Open 70, an intensely exciting but enormously demanding beast of a boat. At 21.5 metres in overall length, overpowered by a cloud of sail and undercrewed by number, the design was potentially the fastest single-hulled sailing vessel the world had seen. From the moment the design parameters emerged, every element of the Volvo Open 70 spelled speed.

The most technologically advanced feature of the design was the canting keel, an appendage attached to the hull by a huge hinge that could swing 40 degrees from the centreline out to the windward side of the yacht. The keel generates the considerable stability needed to counter the pressure of the wind in the sails on these machines. When the yacht goes onto the opposite tack this wing-like fin, which carries a torpedo-shaped lead bulb weighing more than 5 tonnes at its tip, is driven by massive hydraulic rams out to the other side, rams so powerful that they can lift a small commercial jet airliner. Moving the bulb out to windward means the yacht requires less ballast to stay upright than a conventional fin-keeled yacht. For the Volvo Open 70 it means that the power-to-weight ratio—which translates to greater speed—is exceptional. And because a canting keel

spends most of its life canted to windward each yacht carries canards, or fins (usually retractable), just forward of the mast to provide the lateral resistance needed to stop the yacht slipping sideways when sailing across or towards the direction of the wind.

The hull is built as light and strong as possible from carbon fibre with a honeycomb core. Carbon fibre is the material that forms the protective cockpit that saves the lives of Formula One race car drivers when things go horribly wrong and they crash at high speed. That doesn't mean that these yachts are indestructible. A high-speed impact with an unsighted and immovable object lurking on the sea surface—a shipping container, massive log, or small iceberg—could still rip the hull apart like a knife through fabric and immediately imperil the lives of the crew.

"In the Volvo Ocean Race you are all the time pushing to the limit, week after week, around the clock." Mike Sanderson, skipper, *ABN AMRO ONE*

This threat is real, as was graphically illustrated in words by Gordon Maguire, a watch captain aboard *News Corp* in the Volvo Ocean Race 2001–02. They were deep in the Southern Ocean, skirting the Antarctic ice pack between New Zealand and the very sinister Cape Horn, at the southern tip of South America: "The navigator sticks his head up and says 'iceberg on the bow, one mile.' You are sailing under spinnaker at more than 20 knots so you've only got about 3 minutes to get the yacht around it. It's snowing and there's only 400 yards visibility so we are navigating by radar. I need to know if I should go to the left or to the right to miss it. The navigator comes back up and says 'It's on the port bow' then disappears. Then he appears again, 'second iceberg on the starboard bow, half a mile.' I'm saying 'you are kidding me. Is this the same iceberg? Are they joined? This could be one iceberg with two peaks.' I ask: 'What's the gap between them?' It's then too late to go either side. We've got a 'berg to the left, a 'berg to the right and we're going to go through the middle.

The bowman of ABN AMRO TWO holds on tight after the start of leg two from Cape Town to Melbourne.

"One of the younger crew turns round, looks at me and says 'what if they are connected?' I look at him and say: 'Then we're going to die.'"

Why don't they stop? Simple answer: because it is a race—one of the greatest challenges any man, or woman, can face. And they must hold total faith in their yacht and their team.

Like the seafarers who sailed blindly through these icy regions centuries earlier, the Volvo Ocean Race sailors accept the risks. Much of their strength comes from the fact that they are from the elite of the sport and extremely well prepared for every eventuality. It is in the most threatening of situations that their great skill, and that of their teammates, comes into play and will hopefully pull them through. This is the factor that balances the scales between survival and a cogent desire to win.

For ocean-racing sailors, the Volvo Ocean Race represents the pinnacle of achievement. It lures many of the rising stars in offshore racing and international sailors of the highest standing, including Olympic gold

This page, clockwise from left: Dejected crewmember on Brunel *after the luff track on the mast broke on leg two.*

Gerd Jan Poortman, from ABN AMRO TWO, *shows off his wounds after being* swept down the deck in a big seaway.

Near gale conditions on The Solent for the arrival of Brasil 1.

Trying to keep upright as waves wash over the decks of ABN AMRO ONE.

Right: Speeds are starting to climb and spray is flying as the wind and waves pick up for Ericsson.

Far right: A near white-out of water envelopes the crew of ABN AMRO ONE.

medallists, world champions, and America's Cup legends. New Zealand's Mike Sanderson, a seasoned round-the-world campaigner and skipper of *ABN AMRO ONE* explained this magnetic attraction: "There is nothing, absolutely nothing like the Volvo Ocean Race where you race for so long at such high intensity, fully crewed, around the world. It's beyond doing it single-handed—and I've raced single-handed—or two-handed. It's way beyond the challenge of regular races like Sydney to Hobart and Cape Town to Rio because you don't spend as much time at sea with the same team of guys. In the Volvo Ocean Race you are all the time pushing to the limit, week after week, around the clock."

It would be easy to describe the sailors as mad masochists when you consider the self-inflicted punishment they endure. There are two extremes of discomfort for them: the clammy and oppressive tropical heatwaves in the equatorial regions, and the ice-laden blizzards that cut you apart like a thousand razor blades in the bleakest and most foreboding parts of the Southern Ocean. In between these boundaries are gales where the speed of the spray ripping back from the bow hits you like a blast from a fire hose, and the 2-metre-high waves washing down the deck at 30 knots are more difficult to contend with than standing in powerful surf. Then there are the

This would be a game that could not be called off in the event of too much rain, snow, ice, heat, sleet, humidity, or wind. And if the seas rose to the height of 8-storey buildings then so be it.

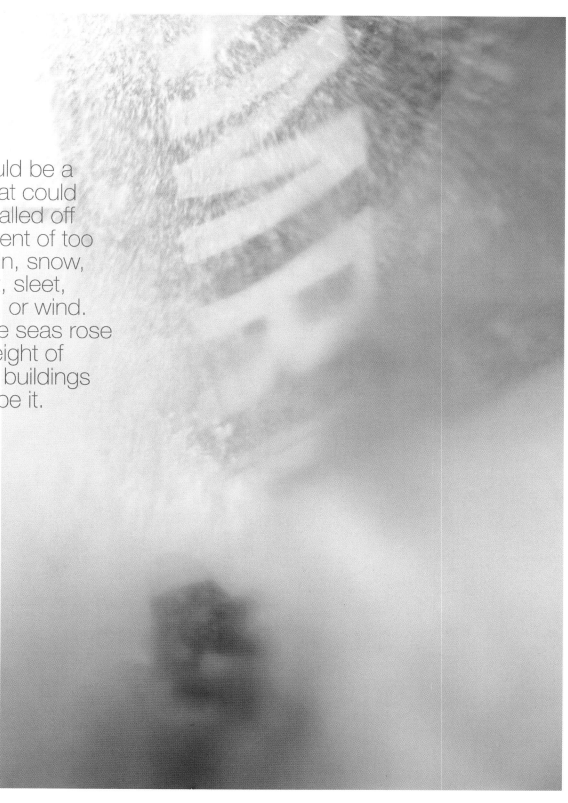

With 50 knots of wind for
Ericsson at Cape Horn,
Damian Foxall clings on.

mind-bending calms where you literally travel at a snail's pace, all the time scanning the sea and the sails, looking to catch that crucial wisp of breeze that might get you moving, and that might also give you a desperately needed break on your rivals. Yes, sailors can actually "see" the wind: a patch of dark ripples on a glassy sea heralds an approaching puff, and the darker the patch the stronger that puff.

The Volvo Open 70 is as spartan as a jail cell, yet it has the functionality of a jet fighter. It is a projectile where there is little consideration for creature comfort and every consideration for speed and minimum weight—an attitude approached with such fanaticism that some crews have been known to cut toothbrush handles in half.

The new rocket ship, the Volvo Open 70, would undoubtedly respond to the slightest gust of wind like no other monohull, all because of its revolutionary design features. On close inspection you realise that this yacht is as spartan as a jail cell, yet it has the functionality of a jet fighter. It is a projectile where there is little consideration for creature comfort and every consideration for speed and minimum weight—an attitude approached with such fanaticism that some crews have been known to cut toothbrush handles in half. The interior is as black as a coal mine: all naked carbon fibre because a can of paint represents additional and unnecessary weight, weight that is better placed in the keel bulb to increase the yacht's stability and its speed potential.

While the boats might be considered large at 21.5 metres in overall length, the living space below deck for the team of 10 is comparable to a yacht half the size, and certainly a lot less comfortable. The claustrophobic main cabin area, where the ceiling is little more than 2 metres above the floor, is your bedroom, bathroom, kitchen, and navigation area. There's no lounge: you're either in the bunk you swap with a man on the opposite watch, or you are on deck. The small floor is covered with a pile of sails (usually wet) and your world is in a state of perpetual motion. Put yourself in a small, dark caravan towed at high speed along a rough road for a few hours and you will begin to get the picture.

But there's more to add to the misery. In the Southern Ocean condensation drips from the ceiling, compounding the water torture, and in the tropics the sweat pours from you in the below-deck sauna.

If you were looking for a rapid-response weight-loss programme it would be hard to beat the Volvo Ocean Race. Crewmembers can lose between

ABN AMRO TWO *is bashed by the waves out in the open sea after the leg three start from Melbourne.*

Left: The rudder of
Brunel cuts through
the water at the start
of leg two.
Right: Bow riding
on board ABN
AMRO TWO.

Crew rarely change clothes: they just add or remove layers according to the conditions. Their wardrobe is very limited because clothes represent weight.

5 and 6 kilograms on some long ocean legs—all due to the diet and the incessant, energy-sapping motion of the yacht. The food is freeze-dried—for breakfast, lunch, and dinner. Yes, the quest for minimum weight and maximum speed even extends to the food, something that makes sense when you consider that thousands upon thousands of dollars are spent on minimising weight in the hull structure. Accordingly, nutritionists play a major role in the race. Their goal is to provide the lightest amount of food possible, but at the same time, deliver the greatest amount of nutrition. Food distribution is controlled by daily ration packs. Each allocation is heated on a tiny, single-burner gas bottle stove in desalinated water—because water tanks and their contents are too heavy.

During the ocean legs the crew splits into two teams that rotate watches every 3 to 4 hours around the clock. If there's a sail to be changed and you're in your bunk then too bad: it's all hands on deck. Rarely do the sailors get more than a couple of hours of unbroken sleep at any one time. If you are below deck, off watch, and the yacht either tacks or gybes then there is a strict procedure to be followed. Apart from helping on deck, every moveable object, including your body, must be transferred to the windward side. And those on deck must manhandle the large and sodden 100-kilo-plus packed sails to the new

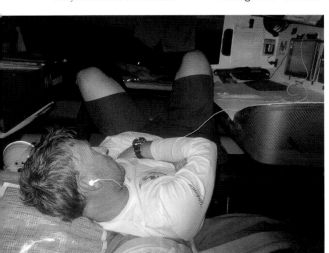

Andrew Cape sleeps on the job on board movistar.

windward side. It's all done to help the yacht's stability: the more upright it remains the more powerful and faster it becomes. Crew rarely change clothes: they just add or remove layers according to the conditions. Their wardrobe is very limited because clothes represent weight. For some, turning underwear inside out after more than a week at sea is seen as a refreshing change. A wash is almost a celebration, and a shower only comes when it rains—if they're lucky and the outside air temperature is conducive to such an activity.

More spice was added to the Volvo Ocean Race 2005–06 with a new course. The yachts would, as usual, follow the traditional routes used by sailing ships of yesteryear when they circumnavigated the globe, harnessing the favourable trade winds and westerly flows that prevail on a course from west to east. But for the first time since its inception as The Whitbread Round The World Race in 1973, this circumnavigation would not start in

For ocean-racing sailors the Volvo Ocean Race represents the pinnacle of achievement. It lures many of the rising stars in offshore racing and international sailors of the highest standing, including Olympic gold medallists, world champions, and America's Cup legends.

the United Kingdom. To take advantage of the opportunity to bring the event to a wider world, the fleet would set sail from Spain, and add four new ports of call—Melbourne, Wellington, New York, and Rotterdam. The UK remained very much in the loop with Portsmouth (host of the start and the finish of the first four Whitbreads) included as a stopover. Another change moved the race finish to the city where Volvo is headquartered, in Göteborg, Sweden.

The most positive and exciting expansion of the game came, however, with the introduction of in-port races, short sprints on the waters of each stopover port. The brainchild of Volvo Ocean Race CEO Glenn Bourke, these races were designed to provide spectators with a ringside view of the amazing yachts and their remarkable crews locked in the heat of battle, something that would make involvement in the Volvo Ocean Race far more valuable for Volvo and the yacht sponsors. The in-port races carried half points towards the overall result, as would the six scoring gates—imaginary lines on the ocean—that each yacht had to cross on the long ocean legs. The point score structure would see the winner of each ocean leg awarded the maximum of seven points, the second yacht would get six, and so on.

The successful introduction of a pitstop in Hobart during the previous Volvo Ocean Race led to two additional pitstops this year: one in Wellington and the other in New York. These brief layovers of between 24 and 48 hours' duration were created to expand awareness of the Volvo Ocean Race with the world media, and to present it to a greater public audience. Each stop would also give sponsors the opportunity to expand corporate hospitality programmes.

The stage was set to make the Volvo Ocean Race 2005–06 the most amazing race around the world, ever!

This page, top: The team from ABN AMRO TWO *wear black bands as a mark of respect to lost crewmate Hans Horrevoets.*

Bottom: Big waves and strong winds as Chris Nicholson trims and Jonathan Swain helms on board movistar.

Meet the Players

Think of today's sporting greats, like Formula One's Michael Schumacher, tennis ace Roger Federer, and football's Ronaldinho.

What do they have to do with the Volvo Ocean Race? Well, the key men who skippered the incredible Volvo Open 70s for the charge around the planet are in a similar league. They are, by far, the world's supreme offshore sailors.

The Volvo Ocean Race is the Grand Prix of challenges when it comes to fully crewed ocean racing, and if you are going to be the best in this competition then you have to be the best at your game before you start. The most credentialed skipper with the strongest team and best-prepared boat would be very hard to beat.

ABN AMRO ONE MIKE SANDERSON

At age 35 Mike "Moose" Sanderson has a list of credits on his sailing CV most professional sailors could not achieve in a lifetime. His first adventures under sail came as a 5-year-old in his native New Zealand, in a tiny Optimist dinghy. His achievements span the America's Cup, Admiral's Cup, short-handed racing, and most of the world's major ocean racing contests. In October 2003 he was a helmsman aboard *Mari Cha IV* when it smashed the transatlantic record and became the first monohull to cover more than 500 nautical miles in a day. As a crewman, he finished first in the 1993–94 Whitbread Race and was second 4 years later. This was his first campaign as a skipper.

ABN AMRO TWO SEBASTIEN JOSSE

Already holding an enviable reputation in the highly competitive world of single-handed sailing, 31-year-old Frenchman Sebastien Josse came into the Volvo Ocean Race as the enthusiastic leader of the youngest team. Major achievements include crewing aboard the maxi catamaran *Orange I* for its record-breaking round-the-world run in 2002, and first place in the Rolex Fastnet Race in 2003. While he might have been short

on experience as the skipper of a fully crewed yacht, Josse's congenial demeanour and determination to succeed made him a logical choice for the role as skipper for this team.

BRASIL 1 TORBEN GRAEL

Most of the crew of *Brasil 1* was new to this type of racing, but what they lacked in offshore miles they certainly made up for with results elsewhere. Torben Grael, 45, is Brazil's most successful Olympic athlete and the world's most successful

Olympic sailor. He has accumulated five medals, including two golds, in six Olympiads, and can also lay claim to six world titles. In total, this remarkable crew holds a staggering array of Olympic medals and 11 world championships between them. Grael is also the only Brazilian to have been part of an America's Cup campaign. With a sailing career that started at age 7, his conquests came across a number of dinghy classes before he progressed into the highly competitive Olympic Star class. His first taste of round-the-world racing was when he joined Knut Frostad aboard *Innovation Kvaerner* for a leg of the 1997–98 Whitbread Race.

BRUNEL GRANT WHARINGTON

It seems that little is impossible for Grant Wharington in the world of yachting. That certainly was the case for this 42-year-old in the build-up to this edition of the Volvo Ocean Race. He overcame a distinct shortage of funds for the Volvo Ocean Race campaign to be in Spain and ready to start—just. His racing credits include line honours in the 2003 Sydney to Hobart Race, victory in the Australian Etchells Championship, and a spectacular win in the 1995 Melbourne to Osaka Race. He was a crewmember on *djuice* in the last Volvo Ocean Race, an experience that made him determined to be here on the line with his own yacht this time.

MATT HUMPHRIES Matt Humphries, 34, took over as skipper of *Brunel* in New York. This was his fourth round-the-world campaign. He started in the 1989–90 Whitbread when, as an 18-year-old, he was the youngest sailor ever to compete.

ERICSSON RACING TEAM NEAL McDONALD

Having stepped aboard *Assa Abloy* as skipper at the end of the first leg of the last Volvo Ocean Race, then sailing it to second place overall, Neal McDonald, 42, came into this edition of the event with every opportunity to go one better. With the planning and talent behind this Swedish-based campaign, the potential was there for the team to be at the top of the podium in Göteborg. Round-the-world racing has been a big part of McDonald's life. As well as completing a Whitbread and Volvo Ocean Race, he was a

crewmember on the catamaran, *Club Med*, when it took out The Race in 2001. McDonald has won the Fastnet and Round Gotland Races, an International 14 world championship, and was on the 1988 British Olympic sailing team.

JOHN KOSTECKI The winner of the last Volvo Ocean Race, John Kostecki, 42, took over as skipper of *Ericsson* for the leg from Rio de Janeiro to Baltimore. He won an Olympic silver medal in 1988, is a 10-time world sailing champion in a variety of classes, and has been associated with four America's Cup campaigns as tactician.

MOVISTAR SAILING TEAM BOUWE BEKKING

The very likable Bouwe Bekking is an amalgam of many nationalities. This 42-year-old was born in Holland, currently resides in Denmark, and participated in this edition of the Volvo Ocean Race under the flag of Spain— not surprising when you realise that for many years he has been a close sailing associate of King Juan Carlos. Bekking's passion for racing around the world came in the 1985–86 Whitbread when, as a 20-year-old, he joined the crew of *Philips Innovator* and finished second. Since then he has raced in most major international events, including nine Admiral's Cup regattas, and become one of the world's most respected offshore sailors. *Movistar* held the world 24-hour sailing distance record going into the race.

PIRATES OF THE CARIBBEAN PAUL CAYARD

In 1998 Paul Cayard, 46, became the first American skipper to win this race, and in so doing set a new standard when it came to preparation, participation, and communication with the outside world. The task looked tougher this time as his yacht was the last to be launched and went into the race almost untried. But the man's talent, and that of the team he assembled, would fill a lot of gaps. He is a seven-time sailing world champion, a five-time America's Cup competitor, and two-time Olympian. He won the coveted Star class world championship in 1988, and in 2002 was elected to the Sailing World Hall of Fame in America. Forever the diplomat, Cayard is very much about the human element of the sport.

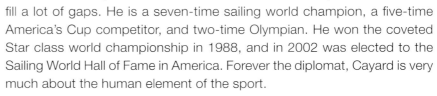

There were many sleepless nights in the Spanish seaside village of Sanxenxo for the CEO of the Volvo Ocean Race 2005–06, Glenn Bourke, during the build-up to the start. Had he made a terrible mistake in his bid to expand the race so it held more appeal to a far larger audience and was truly global in presentation?

He'd moved the start away from its traditional roots in England to the Galicia region on the northwest coast of Spain and things were looking perfect…until 2 weeks before the first round of the contest when horrific late autumn weather arrived. The wind blew at between 40 and 50 knots, the rain was horizontal, and the temperature plummeted to below 10 degrees Celsius. Buildings in the race village were leaking,

TheCont

est

ABN AMRO ONE *in
heavy weather in the
Western Approaches
on leg seven.*

Clockwise from lower left: *Ropes inside their travelling container.*

His Majesty King Juan Carlos of Spain and Volvo Ocean Race CEO Glenn Bourke meet the teams in Sanxenxo, Galicia.

Brasil 1 *is lifted into the water at her christening.*

Movistar *arrives in her home port of Vigo after sailing 5,000 miles from Brazil on her way back from the builders in Australia.*

Ericsson sail testing before the start, off Cape Finisterra near Vigo, Spain.

the electricity was failing, communications were disrupted, and the training schedules for the competing yachts were in chaos. Most worrisome of all? If the weather pattern continued then the much-anticipated throng of spectators would stay away en masse and the start of the new-look Volvo Ocean Race would implode. Four years of intense human endeavour was now held in the palm of a natural force.

As it would turn out, the weather gods were just taunting the Volvo Ocean Race. On the day when all the action began they looked down on the start of one of the world's most incredible sporting contests with benevolence. Bourke and his team could rest more easily.

Still, the race formula had to be proved.

Less than 4 weeks later, at the end of the 6,400-nautical-mile opening ocean leg to Cape Town, there were smiles all round. The formula had already hit its target: The crowds for the opening extravaganza were unprecedented in the 32-year history of the great event, the first ever in-port race had delivered new excitement and opportunities, the ocean leg had seen headline-making high drama and world-record speeds, and the new Volvo Open 70 race yacht had proved to be spectacularly thrilling to watch.

Sanxenxo was going into slumber mode at the end of the summer season when the Volvo Ocean Race came to town. Suddenly, the sleepy village was the focus of attention across the country and around the world. Royalty had come to town, and the media was everywhere—along with 35,000 visitors to watch the in-port race. "Sanxenxo has never seen anything like this in living memory," said one enthusiastic local cab driver. "It is wonderful. Will it come here again?"

Most crews arrived in Sanxenxo at least a month in advance to ready their yachts for the start. The one very obvious absentee was the Australian entry, *Sunergy and Friends*. Rumours accelerated as to whether or not it would actually compete: there was a serious shortfall of funds. It was known

Sanxenxo was going into slumber mode at the end of the summer season when the Volvo Ocean Race came to town. Suddenly, the sleepy village was the focus of attention across the country and around the world.

that the yacht had been shipped from down under to Belgium and was making slow progress south to Sanxenxo in terrible conditions. Then it was suggested that the yacht would merely meet contractual obligations by starting with the fleet, only to withdraw immediately and be shipped home. A one-minute-to-midnight sponsorship deal with two Dutch companies, solar energy giant Sunergy and human resources organisation Brunel, kept the boat in the race. Additional backing from ING Real Estate put enough money in the coffers to race at least as far as Melbourne.

The yacht came over the horizon and into Sanxenxo little more than 24 hours before the start of the in-port race in a raw condition— short of race crew, not officially measured, without its new "racing" keel ballast bulb, minus a complete wardrobe of racing sails, and in need of an overhaul. Competing in the in-port race was out of the question, and it was going to take close to an around-the-clock effort to be ready for the start of leg one from the nearby city of Vigo a week later. For all other participants, preparations were going relatively smoothly considering the weather. *ABN AMRO ONE* did have a personnel problem with valued crewman Mark 'Crusty' Christensen desperately trying to recover from a fractured arm and wrist after a docking accident 2 weeks earlier.

Amazingly, the weather went to the opposite end of the spectrum when it came time for the start of the in-port race. The massive crowd lining the seawalls at the marina, and the waterborne spectators aboard more than 500 widely varying boats, waited more than an hour for sufficient wind to waft across the bay for the competition to commence. Public interest had been enhanced by the presence of royalty: Spain's King Juan Carlos was aboard *movistar* and his daughter, Infanta Doña Cristina, was sailing with *The Black Pearl*, while Volvo Ocean Race patron Prince Carl Phillip of Sweden, was very much enjoying the action aboard Swedish entry, *Ericsson*.

Above: Crowds look down onto the dock before the in-port race in Sanxenxo.

Right: Paul Cayard sets sail from Southampton on the first sea trials with The Black Pearl.

Below: Ericsson sqeezes under the bridge on her way from Green Marine in Lymington, UK, where she was built.

The fleet crosses the start line of the first in-port race in Sanxenxo.

The decision by *Ericsson* skipper Neal McDonald to bring in a hired gun for the day in the form of ace American tactician John Kostecki—winner of the previous Volvo Ocean Race—conveyed the ultimate benefit. The yacht secured the perfect start and quickly sailed away from the rest of the fleet. It was game over and shutters down from that moment, with the Swedish entry cruising to a well-deserved victory ahead of *Brasil 1*, *The Black Pearl*,

Right: The crew of ABN AMRO TWO *drop the spinnaker during the in-port race in Sanxenxo.*

Below: Fireworks finale over Sanxenxo after the finish of the in-port race.

"So often with this race in the past you would sail your guts out and win a leg, but arriving at 2am or even 8pm there's virtually no one there to welcome you, so it doesn't feel like you've won anything. The in-port race makes it like Formula One. You stand up in front of the crowd and you've got the trophy: you're on show and you've got all your buddies around you. It's fantastic." Glenn Bourke, CEO, *Volvo Ocean Race*

movistar, and the two ABN AMRO boats. Many instant experts were quick to point the finger at the ABN teams, saying that they'd made a terrible mistake by leaving the well-worn path to Bruce Farr's design office, instead turning to the little known Argentinean designer, Juan Kouyoumdjian. It was suggested that their boats might be another *djuice*—a non-Farr design that was a big disappointment in the previous Volvo Ocean Race. But if the ABN boys were worried, they certainly didn't show it, stressing all along that this was only the start. The real racing would come on leg one.

For Glenn Bourke the value of the in-port race was all too evident. At the evening dockside presentation of trophies Bourke's smile matched that of McDonald's as the skipper accepted his winner's trophy in front of thousands of enthusiastic spectators. "It exceeded my wildest expectations."

A week later, at the start of leg one from Vigo, Bourke and his management team received an unexpected windfall: "What I didn't realise was that the in-port race would be such a double-whammy for the start of leg one in Vigo; if you didn't know about the race before, then saw all this media coverage about the in-port race you were all of a sudden interested and wanted to be at the start in Vigo. I think that's what happened, that's why we got such an enormous crowd. So, not only was the Volvo Ocean Race start improved upon because it was in a place like Vigo where it was new, vibrant, and exciting, its success was thanks in no small way to the in-port race that had promoted it so powerfully across the board and created such amazing enthusiasm."

"On the first night I think the *movistar* and Pirates crews got frustrated when we blasted through to the lead when it was blowing really hard. They probably said 'we've got to hang onto the ABN guys,' so tried to match us and as a result blew their boats apart." Mike Sanderson, skipper, *ABN AMRO ONE*

Leg01
Vigoto
CapeTown

The largest crowd ever to see a round-the-world race fleet assemble and set sail—some 200,000—made for a remarkable send-off in Vigo. It was a scene made even more special by the presence of the amazing Blue Arrows Spanish Air Force aerobatic team, which performed seemingly death-defying stunts overhead, plus a Spanish Navy aircraft carrier and Sweden's eighteenth-century East Indiaman replica, *Götheborg*. King Juan Carlos, a successful offshore racing yachtsman in his own right, personally said farewell to each crewmember of all competing yachts at dockside before literally leaping aboard the Spanish entry, *movistar.*

Left: The start of leg one of the Volvo Ocean Race in light conditions from Vigo, Galicia.

Above: Ericsson driving hard through the rough seas of the Atlantic on the first leg of the race from Vigo to Cape Town.

Taking the helm, the king guided it away from the dock towards the start area, much to the delight of his adoring public.

Sunergy and Friends, arriving in Vigo scarcely 2 hours before the cannon sounded, made an extremely conservative start; not surprising considering some crew were still all but introducing themselves to others, and they were setting sails they'd not seen before on a boat they'd never sailed. Little more than 24 hours earlier it was discovered that the boat did not measure as a Volvo Open 70 under the class rules—the keel was a scant 2 millimeters out of the required alignment. A frantic overnight modification followed.

The honour of firing the starting canon from the deck of the *Götheborg* was with King Juan Carlos, and when the heavy-sounding thud, accompanied by a thick belch of white smoke, echoed across the waters and through the high hills surrounding Vigo, it was slow-motion sailing beneath a canopy of grey, shower-laden clouds.

The course away from the start line took the fleet to a rounding mark deeper into the bay that Vigo envelopes, then back past the city and on out to sea. *The Black Pearl* started well, but seemingly everyone had their chance for a brief moment of glory. By the time they came back past the Vigo waterfront, through a channel lined by a solid wall of spectator craft, it was pre-race favourite *Ericsson* living up to expectations and showing the way towards the open sea. Fortunately the much-needed breeze arrived with sufficient strength for the Volvo Open 70s to strut their stuff and leave long, vapour trail–like wakes behind them.

With so much having gone into the creation of this edition of the Volvo Ocean Race by shore teams and event management, it was no surprise that the "Thank God They're Gone" party back in Sanxenxo that night was a much-needed release valve. "It had been months and years of grind," said Bourke. "We all enjoyed a few drinks and some good stories, then headed home quite late feeling very happy. Next thing I knew it was just after sunrise and the phone was going: Bang! I had to convince myself I wasn't dreaming. Kimo Worthington, shore manager for *The Black Pearl*, was calling: 'we've got serious problems out there, we're pulling out and trying to get to shore. The boat's in real trouble.' The race was little more than 12 hours old and there was a massive drama. Then half an hour later—BAM!—*movistar*'s in

Hopes for an exhilarating display of high-speed sailing went with the wind—barely enough to hold the 500-square-metre gennakers aloft.

Top: Last minute farewells. Jonelle Christensen hugs husband Mark (Crusty), watch captain on board ABN AMRO ONE, *as daughter Maddy looks on.*

From left: Bowman Tony Kolb climbs Ericsson's *rig to search for wind at the start.*

Movistar *leads* The Black Pearl *round the the first turning mark in Vigo at the start.*

Magnus Woxen tries some video filming on board Ericsson *in the rough seas of the Atlantic.*

Soon there were seven specks on the horizon, their bows by then turned south into the wide open expanse of Atlantic Ocean where howling and hair-raising conditions were waiting. It would be a baptism by fire for this year's racers.

ABN AMRO ONE *sets a new monohull 24-hour world record as they surf through firehosing seas on leg one.*

trouble as well. They had major structural damage but thought they would probably be OK to get back to the coast."

Just prior to having leg one come to a premature end, Cayard and his pirates had seen an astonishing 37 knots on the speedo. At that speed the yacht was careering downwind on the edge of control, launching off waves and crash landing into the trough ahead, something unprecedented in the world of ocean racing. The crash that did the damage led to a fractured bulkhead near the bow, but most threatening to the yacht's safety was the damage around the watertight "fish tank" keel box, which contained the hinge mechanism for the canting keel. Hull fairings (referred to as *bomb doors*) that were designed to keep water pressure in the box to a minimum had been ripped off at high speed. Water was coming into the box at fire-hose pressure and the top of the box was threatening to explode like a burst water hydrant. This would flood the entire centre section of the yacht's

> "The whole boat is shuddering and shaking as we crash through one wave to the next. The winches and blocks are screaming and cracking like cannon fire under the load. Water is pouring down the deck and into the hatch so we have to bail out every half hour. . . This is me at my happiest, tearing through the South Atlantic in excess of 30 knots." Simon Fisher, navigator, *ABN AMRO TWO*

Clockwise from far top:
The Black Pearl *pierces through the rough seas.*
Pepe Ribes at his station on the bow of movistar.
Mark Bartlett prepares to trip the spinnaker on board Sunergy and Friends.

interior. The crew went into action stations, frantically lowering all sails to reduce speed. After assessing the situation the call was to alter course toward Cascais, Portugal. Once there *The Black Pearl* would become one of the world's largest airmail packages: sent in the belly of a massive freight plane to Cape Town where it would be repaired and rejoin the fleet.

Movistar's problem was a little different, but still a "major." Crucial carbon fibre structures supporting the keel control rams had failed and a bulkhead was fractured when the yacht did a horrendous high-speed belly-flop off a wave. *Movistar* would subsequently cruise in to Cape Town as deck cargo on a gargantuan container ship.

Incredibly, on the very first night offshore, the Volvo Ocean Race boats had experienced conditions not dissimilar to what they could expect in the dismal depths of the Southern Ocean. It was a pitch-black night and the seas grew commensurate with the wind—30 knots, 35, 40, and then some. Most remarkable was the form of both TEAM ABN AMRO boats. They had scorched through to leeward of the others doing exactly what every racing sailor dreams of achieving on a downwind leg: sail lower and faster, an

"These new Volvo Open 70s are high-tech machines. They are going to break down. Breaking down is not new to round-the-world racing. We are all learning about what it takes to keep these things together." Paul Cayard, skipper, *The Black Pearl*

Left: A wet ride for the crew on board Brasil 1.
Right: ABN AMRO ONE *ploughs on after passing the scoring gate.*

accomplishment that came through clever sail selection in the form of a "secret weapon"—a tight-luffed reaching headsail that was a cross between a flat-cut genoa and a gennaker. Part of the gain was almost certainly due to the fact that more positive steering was obtained through the fuller hull shape and the twin rudders each design featured.

Hearing of the demise of *The Black Pearl* and *movistar*, Mike Sanderson, skipper of *ABN AMRO ONE*, voiced his theories on what had happened overnight: "They had to watch us come through flat, fast, in control, and comfortably carrying half as much sail again as they were. At times we were a couple of knots faster than the others, and that wouldn't have been good to watch. I think they probably said 'we've got to hang onto the ABN guys,' so tried to match us and as a result blew their boats apart." Already, even this early in the race, Sanderson was starting to feel very comfortable with the design route his syndicate had chosen and the boats they'd built: "Five hours into the leg and I was starting to feel really good. I said to myself, 'hey, we're in this. We can race this race. The boat's certainly fast enough. Yes, we certainly can win the race.' It was a fantastic feeling."

Sanderson wasn't without his own problems that night, though. *ABN AMRO ONE* had to come off the pace for a few hours, the consequence of having speared through a wave that sent a solid, 2-metre-high wall of water cascading aft along the deck with such force that crewmen Tony Mutter and Jan Dekker were washed from their positions and smashed into the leeward helm station. The impact ripped the steering wheel pedestal and other equipment out of the deck and the yacht was knocked flat. The excellent display of seamanship that followed saw the emergency steering put in place and *ABN AMRO ONE* resume racing at 90 percent capacity within 5 hours. Sanderson had expected the incident would cost them between 50 and 60 miles against the fleet, but much to his amazement they were only 5 miles from the lead at the next position report.

Worse was to come for *ABN AMRO ONE*—a sailor's biggest fear outside being lost overboard. Fire! The yacht they called Black Betty because of its dominant hull colour could easily have become "burnt Betty" when a fire broke out in the battery compartment. A bolt dropped into the battery box and lodged between a battery terminal and the carbon fibre structure. Instantly a short circuit blew out the navigation systems, communications, and the onboard media station. Almost as quickly the carbon fibre structure containing the batteries burst into flames. Considering that the entire hull is built from the same highly flammable material, the fire threatened a rapidly accelerating drama. Sanderson grabbed one of his wet socks, held it over his nose as a smoke mask, and attacked the seat of the fire. Crew said later it was possible they had only 5 more seconds to extinguish the flames before they would have been faced with an inferno.

Making the most of the rain: Tony Kolb takes a shower on the deck of Ericsson *as they pass through the Doldrums.*

Chris Nicholson—considered one of the world's best downwind helmsmen—tells what happened aboard *movistar* on the first night out of Vigo.

I was on the helm somewhere between 2 am and 3 am and about 5 minutes before we did the damage we had a 40-knot squall come through. We survived it without any dramas and topped 30 knots at times.

In those conditions you have to be careful when you heat up [change course to increase speed]. I try not to heat her up when we've got a tonne or two of water coming across the deck, so when I knew the deck was dry and things were OK I just heated her up a little bit and she took off: She really had some pace. It was a nice flat section of water and suddenly we were hauling—30 to 32 knots.

I peered ahead and could see a series of three or four bad waves 30 to 40 metres off the bow. We skipped off the first one and landed OK, but things were very different for the next one. Unfortunately, if you wanted to break a boat then this was the perfect wave when it came to length and height to launch from. It was steep and had a perfect angle—everything we didn't want.

There was nothing I could do but try my best to get her over it. The boat felt awkward as she went up, and I knew it was going to be a difficult landing to control because we were going so fast, and this boat likes to misbehave once she sees a bit of air. All I wanted to do was land her flat because it's the safest way: you have your best chance of avoiding a Chinese gybe or broach—both disastrous results. Still, I had another fear that I've always held with these boats—a nosedive and cartwheel. I think that if you get airborne off a big enough wave at 30 knots and land awkwardly on your nose, a cartwheel is a distinct possibility.

So there we were launched, just like a jet taking off. For a split second there was complete and utter silence, other than me saying 'oh dear.' I've no doubt we were fully airborne. Then came the inevitable full-velocity impact. It was like hitting a wall—crash landing, hard, really hard, and flat. The noise was unbelievable—like an explosion.

I was sure we'd dropped the rig because I didn't think anything else could make so much noise when it broke. We got a torch onto the rig and it

"All the guys on deck are staring blankly. A dream has come apart abruptly." Bouwe Bekking, skipper, *movistar*

Clockwise from top: Chris Nicholson concentrates as he drives movistar *hard.*

Russell Bowler, president of Farr Yacht Design, talks with movistar's *skipper Bouwe Bekking as they inspect the damage to the inside of* movistar.

The damage to the hull and daggerboards of movistar *is revealed.*

was fine. Then I really started to worry. I had no doubt we'd done some serious damage so we started looking everywhere on deck. Already everyone had been woken by the noise of the crash and was out of their bunk looking for the damage.

Next I heard a shout with the bad news—we'd (bleep) the keel structure. I can't tell you how bad I felt. I thought about it for 10 seconds: could we keep going? But there was no way. Within 15 minutes we had the sails down and were heading for the coast.

Yet *ABN AMRO ONE* hardly missed a beat on its march south. Sanderson credited legendary round-the-world racing navigator and fellow Kiwi Mike Quilter. "He drummed into us 'Don't let anyone to the west of you,' and that became our game plan. We protected the west. He'd plotted the tracks of most of the previous winners on this leg, and there was definitely a road to follow."

Another early, yet minor casualty on this leg, the Australian entry was forced to change course to Madeira for boom repairs. While it was all but a touch-and-go stop, the Australians would rapidly lose ground on the fleet because, by the time they resumed racing, they'd fallen off the back of the weather system. The wind was then considerably lighter and less favourable in direction.

Two days into the leg, and while riding the best of the weather, "the kids" aboard *ABN AMRO TWO* beat their drum loudest when they became the first yacht in the 32-year history of the event to exceed 500 nautical miles in a day—a stunning effort against the "pros," from a team where the average age was just 26. More remarkable speeds were to come in a seesawing tussle that saw *Brasil 1* leading from *ABN AMRO ONE*, *ABN AMRO TWO*, and *Ericsson*. Things looked evenly balanced as they powered towards the Doldrums, the weather convergence zone near the equator, where good fortune in the form of a beneficial wind zone could make all the difference. This time the equatorial vacuum was almost non-existent and the fleet stayed near to high velocity en route to their first scoring gate, Ilha de Fernando de Noronha, an island off the coast of Brazil. They were at the equator in just 8 days, a performance that would have satisfied sailors of the fastest offshore multihulls just a few years earlier.

With fast downwind conditions continuing in the west it was not surprising to see *ABN AMRO ONE* showing the way "through the gate" at the island and collecting the maximum 3.5 points. Next came *Ericsson*, *Brasil 1*, and *ABN AMRO TWO*. Meanwhile, as these boats made good progress towards their destination, the Australians found the vacuum in the Doldrums that the others missed and soon they were more than 1,000 nautical miles in arrears.

Up front Sanderson's team hooked into an advantageous weather pattern that saw the black boat skip to a healthy lead that was rapidly climbing above 100 nautical miles. Still, the mood was tense. Sanderson correctly predicted that the yacht that sailed the farthest south into favourable westerly winds before turning east towards Cape Town would gain the most—a course that demanded a strong nerve. Despite this, in his opinion, the fleet would

Two days into the leg, and while riding the best of the weather, "the kids" aboard *ABN AMRO TWO* beat their drum loudest when they became the first yacht in the 32-year history of the event to exceed 500 nautical miles in a day.

"It was so serious they were actually considering procedures for abandoning ship. If the keel had broken free, the yacht would have capsized."
Magnus Olsson, syndicate manager, *Ericsson*

Top: ABN AMRO TWO *passes close by the Brazilian island of Fernando de Noronha in second place.*

Inset: ABN AMRO TWO *crosses the equator.*

Below: Hans Horrevoets hard at work with the sewing machine.

soon compress. In *ABN AMRO ONE's* wake only 7 miles separated *Ericsson*, *ABN AMRO TWO,* and *Brasil 1,* the latter making a loss by turning east too early.

Sixteen days into the leg and in perfect downwind sailing conditions, the Volvo Open 70 proved to the world what a breakthrough design it really was. In a 24-hour period both *ABN AMRO ONE* and *ABN AMRO TWO* topped the world-record distance under sail, which had been the 530.19-nautical-mile record established by *movistar* before the start. Sanderson's team achieved 538 nautical miles and Josse, with "the kids," hit 533 nautical miles. "Without a doubt this is definitely life at the extreme," said *ABN AMRO TWO's* navigator, Simon Fisher. "It's a difficult feeling to describe, a mixture of adrenaline and excitement, fear and apprehension. We are pushing the boat to its limit, but it's in control." It wasn't long before *ABN AMRO ONE* raised the height of the bar to a stunning 546 nautical miles, and immediately there was talk of 600 nautical miles in a day being very achievable.

Not so fortunate was the *Ericsson* team, who suddenly found themselves on the brink of a life-threatening drama. *Ericsson* had

been struggling after a spinnaker was lost over the side and a sheet sawed its way deep into the trailing edge of the rudder. The line was eventually cut, but the remnants could not be removed from the rudder blade. Even so they continued sailing at 20 knots towards Cape Town, which was 1,000 nautical miles to the east, until the entire hydraulic system controlling the canting keel suddenly failed. Immediately *Ericsson* was like a bird with a broken wing. The massive appendage had a mind of its own. With each big wave it tried to rip free from its roots, while the hull gyrated wildly around it. Sails were lowered and the yacht stopped so the situation could be assessed.

In a remarkably short time crewman Richard Mason devised a way to control the keel and lock it in the centre of the hull so the yacht could continue sailing at reduced speed. It was an effort that McDonald described as "saving our bacon" when Mason was presented with the Outstanding Seamanship Award in Cape Town.

While *Sunergy and Friends*, later renamed *Brunel*, was never in the hunt for a podium spot on leg one, the yacht's navigator, Campbell Field, kept Volvo Ocean Race followers continually amused with an entertaining array of daily messages from the yacht.

Left: Sunrise on Sunergy and Friends with Jeff Scott at the helm.

Right: Navigator Campbell Field.

This third keel drama brought the canting keel concept even more into question by the media, but equally there were plenty to defend it, especially among race competitors. They were adamant that canting keels represented an exciting and spectacular new era for the sport. It was pointed out that the new Volvo Open 70s were considerably stronger than their predecessor, the Volvo Ocean 60, a class that also had experienced problems when it made its racing debut.

Ericsson crewman Jason Carrington, who was the project manager for the construction of the yacht, explained: "A large powerboat can do 30 knots at sea just like these boats, but you have a throttle to control its speed and to position it on the waves. With these Volvo Open 70s you've got the sails up and you're doing 30-plus knots all the time—there's no throttle you can adjust quickly enough to change the pace. Outsiders find it very easy to criticise a new boat, or a new class, for any race. But also remember, a world record by two boats on the first leg of the Volvo Ocean Race is quite staggering."

Annapolis-based Farr Yacht Design was responsible for four boats in the fleet—*movistar*, *Brasil 1*, *Ericsson*, and *The Black Pearl*. Their thoughts on the dramas came from one of the company's design engineers, Mark Bishop: "We were always used to boats slamming when sailing upwind, but now these boats are going so fast they slam downwind as well, and as a result, the shock loads on the hull, rig, and winches become greatly magnified. The big challenge is for designers to create a structure that can take all the loads and at the same time not be too heavy."

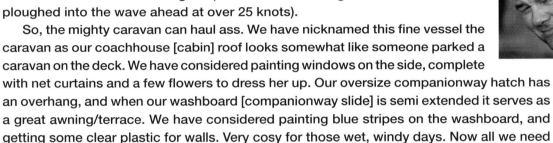

The last 18 to 24 hours have been a hell of a lot of fun . . . a lot learned, not all the hard way. Into the night and our resident specialists Scotty (Jeff Scott) and Barney (Ian Walker) started their 4x4 driving, showing the rest of us how it is done, with sustained boat speeds of over 25 knots, peaking into the 30s—basically the best sailing you will ever get on a monohull. Fraser (Brown), who has been around the world twice on maxi multihulls was sitting back the whole time yawning his head off. The rest of us had ear-to-ear grins (with the occasional grimace thrown in as we ploughed into the wave ahead at over 25 knots).

So, the mighty caravan can haul ass. We have nicknamed this fine vessel the caravan as our coachhouse [cabin] roof looks somewhat like someone parked a caravan on the deck. We have considered painting windows on the side, complete with net curtains and a few flowers to dress her up. Our oversize companionway hatch has an overhang, and when our washboard [companionway slide] is semi extended it serves as a great awning/terrace. We have considered painting blue stripes on the washboard, and getting some clear plastic for walls. Very cosy for those wet, windy days. Now all we need are a couple of plastic chairs. This has given birth to a new vocabulary:

A bit more weight needed on the tow hitch = move some weight forward

Too much weight on the tow hitch = the bow is going in [nosediving]

We have a flat tyre = the steering is getting very heavy

The mudflaps are working well = nice and dry ride when going fast

Close to jack-knifing here boys = no prizes for figuring that one out [a broach]

Turn the taillights on = navigation lights

Brake lights on please = Turn on the instrument lights please

Wheel bearings need some work = one of our rudders is starting to ventilate

It goes on and on. I'm not even sure if anyone but us finds this amusing. We may be going a little mad out here. Anyway, *Brasil 1* has finished, so just the two of us left. *Ericsson* will be in soon, and we will be all on our own. I am wondering how I am going to manage the daily inter-fleet radio sched with myself. I'll probably get a few strange looks from the others if I sit down in the nav station and call on the SSB radio '*Sunergy and Friends, Sunergy and Friends,* this is *Sunergy and Friends*, please confirm that all is OK on board.' I might have to do without external contact for a few days; otherwise I might find myself confined to my bunk and heavily sedated.

Come to think of it that's not a bad option. If you don't hear from me in 24 hours, you know what has happened.

"The fleet had had the life kicked out of it by the weather, and boats were breaking. For a moment I thought it was the worst thing that could have happened, then I realised that it was probably the best thing in the world for the race. The boats would be stronger and safer for the remaining legs, and the crews would know what they were dealing with in this new design." Glenn Bourke, CEO, Volvo Ocean Race

ABN AMRO ONE wins leg one.

Inset: Mike Sanderson jubilant on the podium after winning leg one.

More surprises were on hand, most surprisingly from the team from down under. Even though they were trailing the others by around 1,500 nautical miles, the Australian team was still pushing hard, so hard in fact that they recorded the highest 6-hour run for any yacht on the leg—an average of 23 knots, which, if they'd been able to maintain for 24 hours, would have seen them better 550 nautical miles. Unfortunately any chance they had of making a charge towards *ABN AMRO ONE*'s world distance record ended when a large hull fairing at the root of the keel ripped off. From that moment they may as well have been dragging a bucket. Still, they managed to become only the fifth yacht on the planet to top 500 nautical miles in 24 hours, an achievement that meant four of the five fastest yachts in the world were Volvo Open 70s. The fifth, *Mari Cha IV*, which covered 525.7 nautical miles in 2003, is twice their length. Ironically, Mike Sanderson and three of his *ABN AMRO ONE* crew were aboard for that run.

With Cape Town's towering Table Mountain looming large in the background, capped by its cloth of cloud, an elated Sanderson guided *ABN AMRO ONE* across the finish line off the city's waterfront almost 19 days to the minute after departing Vigo. Surrounded by family, friends, and well-wishers at the dockside trophy presentation, with champagne arcing through the air, he sang the praises of his crew, shore team, and designer. For him his boat's critics had been answered in a most emphatic fashion. "TEAM ABN AMRO has worked so hard for this," he said. "Before we started we were told by our designer, Juan Kouyoumdjian, that we would average 16 knots on this leg and we all laughed. We have averaged 15.95 knots and put in nearly 400 miles almost every day of this leg." It was only the second time in 20 years that a non-Farr-designed yacht had won a leg of the race, something that eased a nagging worry the skipper held deep from the outset: "Every time someone has ventured off the mark when it came to design they've been caught short. I have to admit that I wondered if we might have had another *djuice* on our hands. You just never know until you race."

From left: Skipper of Brasil 1, *Torben Grael*, draped in the Brazilian flag, is applauded by navigator Adrienne Cahalan.

Sebastien Josse, skipper of ABN AMRO TWO, chats to the media on the dockside.

ABN AMRO TWO *ghosts into Cape Town in very light winds against the fading light.*

Richard Mason with his young daughter on board Ericsson *soon after the boat arrived in Cape Town.*

Just six-and-a-half hours later the rank outsiders, "the kids," arrived in Cape Town, and if you hadn't known any better, you would have guessed by the euphoria surrounding them that they'd actually won. It was a sensational effort from the youngest and least-experienced team in the race. "The atmosphere on board has been fantastic," said a beaming navigator, Simon Fisher. "We can't say that we haven't beaten ourselves from pillar to post, but at least we managed to do it with a smile on our faces. To get second is just an awesome job."

Nine hours later Torben Grael sailed *Brasil 1* across the line. It had been a frustrating finish, taking 7 hours to cover the last 20 nautical miles after a high-speed run all the way from Vigo. Navigator Adrienne Cahalan, who had sailed five previous round-the-world campaigns, was already looking forward to the next leg, to her favourite place on the planet: "The Southern Ocean is its own animal. We had a little taste of it on the way here. Preparation is the key to the Southern Ocean and we will need to get our minds focused and re-programme ourselves to think about the cold air."

Sadly "cold air" wasn't to be a problem for Adrienne. A few days after arriving in Cape Town she was off the crew on the grounds that these boats were, as Kiwi race-veteran Jeff Scott would suggest at the end of the leg, man-eaters. The boats needed all the brute strength they could muster, and she just wasn't strong enough. It appeared to be a surprising decision from the *Brasil 1* camp considering that she had trained with them for so long.

The dismissal meant that for the first time in the 32-year history of this contest, a leg of the course would be an all-male affair.

Leg 1 Results

Leg Position	Yacht	Elapsed Time	Leg Points	Sanxenxo In-Port Race Points	Scoring Gate Points	Overall Points	Overall Standing
1	ABN AMRO ONE	19d 00h 24m	7.0	1.0	3.5	11.5	1
2	ABN AMRO TWO	19d 6h 56m	6.0	1.5	2.0	9.5	4
3	Brasil 1	19d 15h 58m	5.0	3.0	2.5	10.5	2
4	Ericsson	20d 16h 47m	4.0	3.5	3.0	10.5	2
5	Sunergy and Friends	24d 1h 33m	3.0	0.0	1.5	4.5	5
6	The Black Pearl	did not finish	1.0	2.5	0.0	3.5	6
7	movistar	did not finish	1.0	2.0	0.0	3.0	7

"In the Southern Ocean big waves will present bigger problems, especially at night. If you go charging down a huge swell and there's another wave on the face of that wave, then there's a good chance that you'll skip off it, get airborne and land on your nose. Who knows what will happen after that, but there's a chance you will cartwheel." Chris Nicholson, watch captain, *movistar*

Cape Town to Melbourne

The alarming presence of icebergs well north of their usual habitat near Antarctica saw Chris Nicholson's fears somewhat allayed. Considering the threat that these massive 'bergs posed to the yachts, the race organisers, skippers, and navigators met and agreed unanimously to set a limit on how far south the fleet could sail. They established two 500-nautical-mile-long "ice gates" at 42 degrees south—imaginary lines in the water at approximately the same latitude as the southern tip of Tasmania. The yachts had to keep these safety barriers to the south of their 6,100-nautical-mile track between Cape Town and Melbourne.

Any competitors who felt they would miss out on all the exciting action of the

Left: Movistar, Ericsson, and ABN AMRO TWO battle upwind during the in-port race in Cape Town.

Above: Driving hard on board ABN AMRO TWO.

deep south were wrong, very wrong. By Melbourne there was no doubt that the new Volvo Open 70s were the most exciting long-distance offshore racing monohulls the world had seen. In the 12 weeks since Vigo they had monstered the world 24-hour sailing distance record not once, but three times! Approaching Australia the "kids" showed little sense of fear when they drove *ABN AMRO TWO* to a stunning new world mark of 563 nautical miles—up an impressive 33 nautical miles on the record that was in place when the Volvo Ocean Race started. It was a performance that reignited speculation that a previously inconceivable 600-nautical-mile-plus 24-hour run was distinctly possible before the race ended in Göteborg. That would be the equivalent of breaking the 4-minute mile.

A foretaste of what lay ahead came on the day of the in-port race in Cape Town—40 knots of wind howling offshore that whipped the waters of Table Bay into a frenzy of white foam and block-like seas.

During the 5-week stopover in Cape Town there was little time for crews to rest and enjoy the magnificent natural attributes of the region: work needed to be done. The structural and keel hydraulic problems that impacted the first stage needed to be eliminated. Not even the overall leader, *ABN AMRO ONE*, had escaped unscathed from the hammering on leg one. While that team's boatbuilders dealt with delamination on the hull, Mike Sanderson and his riggers fitted their largest headsail to a roller furler—an apparatus that would allow them to quickly and efficiently roll the sail up like a giant Holland blind whenever the yacht was overpowered by the wind while careering across the Southern Ocean. It was a bowman's dream come true: he no longer needed to go onto the foredeck in rugged weather to lower the sail.

Meanwhile a small element of doomsayers outside the race were quick to declare the Volvo Open 70 too dangerous for the Southern Ocean. Their calls fell apart when only two of the 70 competitors in the race withdrew

Far left: Light winds plague the fleet as they drift towards the start of leg two in Table Bay.

Inset: Brasil 1, *fully powered up during the Cape Town in-port race.*

in Cape Town, and not necessarily out of a fear about the boats or the dangers associated with the course down south. But Southern Ocean phobia can strike a crew suddenly, as at the start of the leg south from Punta del Este in the 1993–94 race when one sailor, at the very last moment, chose home over the high seas. He was aboard *Uruguay Natural*, and as it manoeuvred for the start, thoughts of freezing temperatures, icebergs, gales, and massive waves overwhelmed him. He jumped overboard and, with flaying arms, swam for shore.

For this race though, everyone was ready to go for what would probably be the ride of their lives . . . surfing the world's fastest monohulls down massive seas at speeds they'd never previously considered possible.

Clockwise from left: Movistar *crew hard at work at the start of leg two.*

Movistar *wipes out at the gybe mark during the in-port race.*

ABN AMRO TWO *creeps up on* Ericsson *at the start of leg two.*

A foretaste of what lay ahead came on the day of the in-port race in Cape Town—40 knots of wind howling offshore that whipped the waters of Table Bay into a frenzy of white foam and block-like seas. *ABN AMRO ONE* scorched around the 25-nautical-mile track in a brilliant display of heavy-weather, high-speed sailing. While the opposition languished in *ABN AMRO ONE's* wake—gyrating wildly out of control through gybes, running aground, and being knocked down—the Sanderson team sailed their yacht with apparent ease, surging downwind in a cloud of spray at better than 30 knots. This was a rare day in international keelboat

racing where crowds actually cheered while watching the excitement unfold before their eyes. *ABN AMRO ONE* cruised home almost 7 minutes ahead of *movistar*, which led the very determined youngsters aboard *ABN AMRO TWO*.

When it came to start time for leg two, it was as if Cape Town did not want to release the fleet. The waters of Table Bay were glassy and the flags on the committee boat flopped around flaccidly in the gentle ocean swell. There was barely a breath of wind. Even the usual cloth of cloud was missing from the sun-drenched top of Table Mountain. The impressive spectator fleet, numbering in the hundreds, was dominated by a South African naval frigate that demonstrated its support for the race by carrying a large blue Volvo logo on the side of its battleship-grey superstructure.

It took the yachts nearly 2 hours to claw their way up the 2-mile leg to the offshore turning mark where the contest became very entertaining—for the spectators. With only the slightest breath of air, and an adverse current coming into play, it was a chaotic scene as the yachts tried to round the mark as one. There were bangs, bashes, crashes, bent railings, frayed tempers, and protest flags as desperate moves to clear the mark continually failed. Eventually the faintest breeze arrived to carry the yachts south, past the most southwestern corner of the South African continent, the Cape of Good Hope. But rather than the much-desired westerly winds, southeasterlies and nasty head seas dealt severe punishment.

> Eventually the faintest breeze arrived to carry the yachts south, past the most southwestern corner of the South African continent, the Cape of Good Hope.

Damian Foxall on the boom of Ericsson.

Once past the Cape of Good Hope, *movistar* began living up to the expectations it held pre-race by taking the lead on a more northerly course than the others. However, they ended up too far north for the emerging weather pattern and could only watch the opposition slip through to the south. Much to everyone's delight, a real race unfolded with *Ericsson*, *The Black Pearl,* and *Brasil 1* proving competitive against the two ABN AMRO boats. At the same time Grant Wharington's under-developed Australian entry was not surprising anyone by bringing up the rear.

Less than 300 nautical miles out from Cape Town the scene suddenly changed when first *Ericsson* and then *Brasil 1* reported serious problems. *Ericsson* was returning to port with more keel hydraulic problems—a broken ram—while Torben Grael radioed that his yacht was turning back because of a major structural failure in the deck near the mast. *Ericsson* would arrive in Melbourne on a container ship while a repaired *Brasil 1* set off in pursuit of the fleet almost a week later.

Crews did not taste the worst extremes of the deep south, but the new course and the energy-sapping speed of these boats still placed every possible physical and mental demand

Clockwise from left: Brunel *sails into the setting sun after passing the Cape of Good Hope.*

The cold sets in on The Black Pearl *as the team heads for the Southern Ocean.*

A lonely albatross glides the waves. Welcome to the Southern Ocean.

A whale sleeps on the surface in the path of The Black Pearl.

The Plight of the Albatross

The magnificent albatross is the guardian of the Southern Ocean, the major field of play in the Volvo Ocean Race.

Since ancient times these large and superbly proportioned white birds with black-tipped wings have been a symbol of life for mariners who have ventured into this most powerful and threatening region that rings Antarctica. In that time, the albatross has become the font of great legends, including a belief that each one carries the souls of seafarers who have perished there.

Few birds can match the albatross when it comes to aerodynamic efficiency. Their very long and narrow wings, which can span 3 metres, allow them to travel up to 10,000 kilometres at a time, primarily through the use of an energy-saving technique called dynamic soaring.

It is enthralling to see them fly so effortlessly and majestically, all the time riding the vertical wind gradient, the updraft, generated across the face of a moving wave.

Sadly, though, this is becoming an increasingly rare sight. These birds, with origins dating back around 50 million years, are seeing their existence being threatened in a blink. In just 3 decades all 21 albatross species have become endangered, primarily because of longline fishing.

It is an ecological tragedy that demands international action, and most appropriately the Volvo Ocean Race opted to support the Save the Albatross campaign initiated by Birdlife International and the Royal Society for the Protection of Birds.

Longliners set up to 10,000 baited hooks at a time on a single line stretching more than 100 kilometres. All too often, as these baits enter the water, albatross unwittingly seize them before they sink and are then dragged underwater to drown. It was estimated that during the 7 months the Volvo Ocean Race took to complete some 60,000 albatross died needlessly because of longlining.

In lending their support to the Save the Albatross campaign, Volvo Ocean Race organisers and competitors hoped that they could accelerate the awareness of the plight of the albatross. Like all other supporters of the effort, they wanted to impress upon fishermen that there are relatively simple solutions available. Research has shown that albatross mortality can be dramatically reduced through the setting of longlines at night when the birds are not active, or by adding additional weight on the lines so the baits sink far more quickly. Flying long streamers from the back of the vessel also keeps the birds away from the baits while they sink.

Hans Horrevoets and
Simeon Tienpont hard
at work repairing sails
on ABN AMRO TWO.

in their way. Mike Sanderson struggled with an earlier proclamation that they would hold back at times to preserve the boat: "Currently at the frantic pace of our 24-hour record run [on the first leg], just as I am typing here, the speed hits 27 knots . . . masthead 'chute, full mainsail, big staysail . . . pitch black. Oh yeah, we know all about backing off."

By day nine it was all *ABN AMRO ONE*. Having been first to escape a high-pressure system, the Dutch boat went from a 16-nautical-mile advantage to a massive 380-nautical-mile lead in just 4 days. Being first to pass the Kerguelen Islands, she took the maximum 3.5 points that were available. This was the first of the two scoring gates on the leg.

The strong winds on approach to the Kerguelens and the charge being made by the "kids" in second place refocused world attention on the race. Simon Fisher said it all: "If the conditions we had yesterday put the smiles back on everyone's faces, then today

This would probably be the ride of their lives . . . surfing the world's fastest monohulls down massive seas at speeds they'd never previously considered possible.

Clockwise from top: Brasil 1 *is dismasted and a jury rig is made.*
ABN AMRO TWO *breaks another world record.*
The mast and sail of Brasil 1 *floats just below the surface.*
Brasil 1 *surfing before she is dismasted.*
A jubilant crew on ABN AMRO ONE *passes Eclipse Island.*

has sent the grins from ear to ear. It has been a very special day for us so far, as we have broken new ground and taken a monohull past the 550-mile mark in 24 hours. Better still, just minutes ago, I received a message from race headquarters saying we had raised the bar to 563! The boys are ecstatic!"

Luke Molloy told of the intoxicating excitement and adrenaline rush that came when steering the new world record holder in those conditions: "There is something exhilarating about blasting through waves in the darkness of night with very little guidance, but for some instrument numbers illuminated on the mast. As the boat skips along through 25, 28, 30 knots, my grip on the wheel tightens, my knees bend and my body tenses up a little because my gut instinct senses the inevitable . . . Nosedive! 31, 32 knots and BOOF! We are jolted forward like we have hit a brick wall then smashed back

"Twenty-five knots and a very short and sharp chop made going upwind pretty bloody awful! For most people the constant pounding caused most stomachs to be set on spin cycle. Sleeping was not a lot of fun either, as every other wave tossed you in the air like a pancake. The only way to sleep was to hold on as tightly as you could to the bunk—meaning you couldn't actually sleep because you were holding on so hard!!" Simon Fisher, navigator, *ABN AMRO TWO*

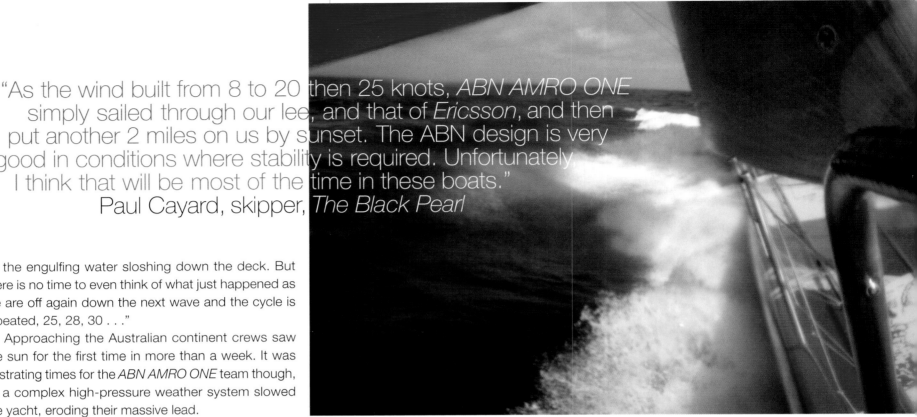

"As the wind built from 8 to 20 then 25 knots, *ABN AMRO ONE* simply sailed through our lee, and that of *Ericsson*, and then put another 2 miles on us by sunset. The ABN design is very good in conditions where stability is required. Unfortunately, I think that will be most of the time in these boats."
Paul Cayard, skipper, *The Black Pearl*

Right: The Black Pearl scorches through the Southern Ocean.

Below: Bouwe Bekking hugs his daughter on arrival in Melbourne.

by the engulfing water sloshing down the deck. But there is no time to even think of what just happened as we are off again down the next wave and the cycle is repeated, 25, 28, 30 . . ."

Approaching the Australian continent crews saw the sun for the first time in more than a week. It was frustrating times for the *ABN AMRO ONE* team though, as a complex high-pressure weather system slowed the yacht, eroding their massive lead.

They were relieved to take the second lot of mid-course points that were available at Eclipse Island, located just 1.5 nautical miles off the southern coast of Western Australia. From there they only needed to cover the opposition to lead into Melbourne, still 1,300 nautical miles to the east. But no one told the "kids" that, and, by midway across the Great Australian Bight, *ABN AMRO TWO* had made huge gains, trailing their teammate by a mere 30 nautical miles. At one stage they were just 16 nautical miles behind.

It was down to that pair to sort out the top two spots on the podium as both *movistar* and *The Black Pearl* had been "winged"—slowed yet again by structural and hydraulic keel ram problems. Both pulled into the old whaling town of Albany, on the coast near Eclipse Island, to make temporary repairs. Bouwe Bekking left no doubt about his anger: "In Melbourne we will rip these [rams] out and send them back to the manufacturer (MONEY BACK!!) and put our stainless steel ones back in *movistar*."

Meanwhile, the "Aussie Battlers" aboard *ING Real Estate Brunel*, formerly named *Sunergy and Friends*, pushed on doggedly

despite trailing more than 1,000 nautical miles. Much of their deficit came when they lost time with a sail problem—a gennaker wrapped around the keel and rudders—and they missed a favourable weather system.

Brasil 1, back at sea after making repairs, pressed on, 2,000+ nautical miles behind the leader. They were inspired by a personal message from the President of Brazil, Luiz Inácio Lula da Silva, which said in part: "I want to congratulate skipper Torben Grael and his entire *Brasil 1* team for returning to the Volvo Ocean Race regatta. The persistence that the Brazilians have shown, even after a series of problems, proves that we are a nation that never gives up." Inspired as they were, there was nothing they could do when, 1,300 nautical miles southwest of Perth, Western Australia, their world came crashing down around their ears. A fitting on the mast broke and the massive carbon fibre structure exploded into three pieces. The yacht made it to Perth under jury rig, then to Melbourne across thousands of kilometres of Australian continent on the back of a huge truck.

After 19 days at sea Sanderson's team overcame a frustratingly light final few hundred miles to arrive first into Melbourne and in doing so, consolidated their position at the top of the points table. Equally impressive though was Sebastien Josse and the kids. Still full of fight, they sailed *ABN AMRO TWO* home just 4 hours in arrears, and to cap off the celebrations they had the 24-hour record in the bag. Rank outsiders at the start of this contest, it had to be agreed that what they lacked in age and long-distance ocean racing experience was balanced, in no uncertain fashion, by great skill, determination, and youthful exuberance. The wounded warriors, *movistar* and *The Black Pearl*, battled their way home to take third and fourth place while *ING Real Estate Brunel* arrived a distant fifth.

The crews were quick to counter the controversy about the safety and seaworthiness of the Volvo Open 70. Mike Sanderson declared: "The world called for a grand prix boat, the world got a grand prix boat, and now everyone had better not complain about it. A fantastic race boat has been delivered here and you make of the rule what you want: it is not anyone else's fault. We have just got to work out what pace you can drive a Volvo Open 70."

The always-eloquent Paul Cayard added: "If life was all smooth sailing it would not be worth living. We need some challenges in order to feel we are conquering something. I would not want to be sitting behind some desk somewhere, criticizing people who are willing to 'dig deep' to cross into new territory. As far as I can remember, there aren't a lot of points of land or holidays named after people who sat at home and criticised Christopher Columbus."

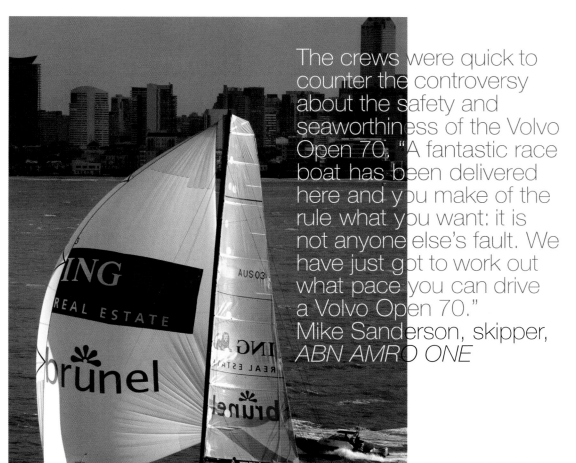

The crews were quick to counter the controversy about the safety and seaworthiness of the Volvo Open 70. "A fantastic race boat has been delivered here and you make of the rule what you want: it is not anyone else's fault. We have just got to work out what pace you can drive a Volvo Open 70."
Mike Sanderson, skipper, ABN AMRO ONE

From left: Mike Sanderson celebrates another win.

ING Real Estate Brunel heads into Melbourne to finish fifth.

Leg 2 Results

Leg Position	Yacht	Elapsed Time	Leg Points	Cape Town In-Port Race Points	Scoring Gate 1 Points	Scoring Gate 2 Points	Previous Points	Overall Points	Overall Standing
1	ABN AMRO ONE	18d 22h 8m	7.0	3.5	3.5	3.5	11.5	29.0	1
2	ABN AMRO TWO	19d 2h 20m	6.0	2.5	3.0	3.0	9.5	24.0	2
3	movistar	19d 14h 50m	5.0	3.0	2.0	2.5	3.0	15.5	3
4	The Black Pearl	21d 1h 24m	4.0	1.5	2.5	2.0	3.5	13.5	5
5	ING Real Estate*	21d 10h 42m	3.0	0.5	1.5	1.5	4.5	11.0	7
6	Brasil 1	did not finish	1.0	2.0	1.0	0.0	10.5	14.5	4
7	Ericsson	did not finish	1.0	1.0	0.0	0.0	10.5	12.5	6

*ING Real Estate Brunel *was withdrawn after leg two and re-entered the competition as* Brunel *in the USA.*

"It's not just a race but also an adventure, an extreme sport, and the cheapest way I could find to travel the world. On this journey I am lucky enough to have a great group of friends who are extremely talented. Having a crew from seven nations leaves never a dull moment on deck, with constant banter from culture to music, movies, language, and comparisons from all angles of our similar but different lives." Luke Molloy, crew, *ABN AMRO TWO*

Leg03
Melbourne to Wellington

43

It was crunch time during the stopover in Melbourne; crunch time when it came to solving the problems associated with the canting keel systems. *Movistar* skipper Bouwe Bekking had earlier summed up the thinking: "How did we manage to sail 20,000 miles in training without having real problems with the hydraulics? Answer: they were nearly double the weight with a less pressurized system, and I changed them for the 'performance' gain to be had. We will put our stainless steel hydraulics back in—at least we will then be able to sail the boat full throttle . . . and sleep a little better when off-watch."

With many campaigns struggling because of these problems, outside the

Left: A bumpy ride for The Black Pearl as she sails through Melbourne Heads on her way to Wellington.

Above: Gerd Jan Poortman is confined to his bunk after injuring his back in the heavy seas.

Brasil 1 *was nicknamed "Brasilia, Queen of the Desert" after a 4,000-kilometre journey from Western Australia to Melbourne on a low-loader truck.*

Experts were brought in from around Australia and overseas to help, and, in a real display of camaraderie, there was much sharing of information between teams. While the frantic repair work took place, more than 300,000 people enjoyed the carnival atmosphere at Melbourne's Waterfront City precinct at Docklands where the race village was located. The Volvo Ocean Race yachts were a focus of attention in what all agreed was an ideal stopover facility.

There was one very notable absentee among the boats: *Brasil 1*. Under special escort, she was travelling the 4,000 kilometres from Perth across the arid, ochre-coloured Australian desert and through the outback to Melbourne. Her "skipper" for this 4-day journey was Charlie Mills, a very likeable rogue with vast experience when it came to transporting difficult loads like this. Even so, the *Brasil 1* job did give him a slight case of the jitters: "I've never seen one of these so close, and I thought 'hell, it's bigger than they look on the sea. This is going to be a bit of a problem.' Then when I found out how much the thing cost I nearly fell over backwards."

The load was 27 metres long, 5.1 metres wide, and 5 metres high. During the drive Charlie had to avoid oncoming traffic, roadtrains, power lines, and tight corners. He also had to try to stay on solid ground and make sure the boat didn't get damaged by stones thrown up from the road by passing vehicles. In Melbourne Charlie was a star. He had never seen anything quite like the media interest in his efforts. Photographs of "Brasilia, Queen of the Desert" making its passage on the back of his truck appeared in newspapers and magazines around the world.

With *Brasil 1* arriving only a couple of days before the in-port race in Melbourne, it was an around-the-clock effort to replace the mast and have the boat ready to race. Even as the yachts were departing the dock for the course on Port Phillip Bay, skipper Torben Grael wasn't certain of starting. He feared that the new mast might break if a temporary fitting failed. As it was, the hastily prepared *Brasil 1* almost delivered a fairytale result in front of more than 1,000 spectator boats, leading for more than half the distance before yet another keel hydraulic failure forced her back to fifth. It was a race that saw controversy when *ABN AMRO TWO* and *Ericsson* were recalled for jumping the gun, and then offered the closest in-port competition so far. *ABN AMRO ONE* was the winner over *The Black Pearl* and *movistar*.

Wellington was only a pitstop at the end of leg three, meaning the boats would stay there only 2 or 3 days before sailing to Rio de Janeiro. Race rules stipulated that no additional equipment, including food, could be taken on

race the canting keel generated considerable ill-informed controversy. CEO Glenn Bourke called a meeting with the race skippers, key crewmembers, and designers to discuss the major issues, and to ask if changes needed to be made to the Volvo Open 70 rules. Much to Bourke's delight the teams were unanimous in their belief that the root of the structural and hydraulic problems lay within their own campaigns, and it was their responsibility to do something about it. The clear message was, "nobody knows what's happening to us out there better than we do, so please leave it in our hands."

"This race tests many facets of your personality. Being thrown around continuously, getting cold and wet with not enough sleep or food are all easily understood and very hard on the body. But the mental stress is something that is harder to describe, and often much harder to deal with than the physical discomforts."
Steve Hayles, navigator, *Ericsson*

board there. Violators of this rule would incur a 2-hour time penalty at the start of leg four. Accordingly all yachts were laden to the gunwales leaving Melbourne, with everything required for the following 8,000 nautical miles.

When it came to the start of the 1,450-nautical-mile leg to Wellington there was again around 1,000 spectator boats on Port Phillip Bay. One boat was missing from the fleet, the horribly uncompetitive *ING Real Estate Brunel.* Skipper Grant Wharington opted to make drastic modifications to the yacht in his home port, then ship it to Baltimore to rejoin the race.

The profile of the bay is the shape of a balloon with a large body of water and a very narrow entrance. The 25-nautical-mile route from the start near the city, to the tricky, tidal-influenced entrance to the south, saw the yachts sail into a vacuum of no breeze at the halfway stage. Eventually, when the seabreeze arrived, they made a spectacular exit, bucking their way through short, steep seas and throwing up clouds of spray. It was a wet welcome to the infamous Bass Strait. *ABN AMRO ONE* led a tightly bunched pack when they turned southeast towards New Zealand.

The ride through the night, out of Bass Strait into the Tasman Sea, was wild. Sebastien Josse reported from *ABN AMRO TWO* that their situation on board was "horrendous." They'd torn their mainsail, lost all power to the boat at one stage, and had bowman "Johnny" Poortman injured and in his bunk after he was smashed by a savage wave. It would be realised in Wellington that Poortman's injuries were worse than first thought. He explained what happened: "I went forward to check on damaged stanchions and lifelines when we stuck the bow into a wave while doing more than 20 knots. I was attached by my safety harness, but the wave that came down the deck still smashed me into the daggerboard. I found myself wrapped around it, with the board between my legs, not able to move. The impact dislocated my

Left: The Black Pearl bowman prepares to spike the spinnaker.
Top: Tom Braidwood, huddled and exhausted on board Ericsson on day four.
Bottom: Bouwe Bekking drives movistar through heavy seas.

Brasil 1 *blasts towards Wellington.*

The Sailing "Circus"

It would be easy to focus only on the competing yachts when considering the title, The Volvo Ocean Race Round the World. After all, it's simply a competition where the yachts set sail from one port and hightail it to the next—or is it?

The fact is there was another huge and extremely vital part of the Volvo Ocean Race event that few people saw, one that could be likened to a travelling circus that stayed with the race from start to finish.

It was a "circus" with many facets, including:

• The organisers—event management, race management, and the media team;

• Yacht support teams—the men and women who work behind the scenes like a pit crew in a motor race. They include sailmakers, engineers, boat maintenance specialists, media teams, and syndicate management;

• Race and syndicate sponsors—starting with Volvo and including associate sponsors of the event and the sponsors backing each team.

Each group had an enormous amount of equipment associated with it, from inflatable race management boats and course rounding marks to mobile workshops and sail lofts, as well as massive display stands and portable hospitality pavilions—and the lot had to be moved from one port to another.

The smaller items were air freighted, but because of the sheer size of the largest structures there was not sufficient time for them to be dismantled, shipped by sea to the next port, and reassembled before the yachts arrived. This meant that each group needed two of each of these items, all part of what was a giant leapfrog project around the planet. For example, the largest display stands and hospitality pavilions seen at the start in Sanxenxo were next used in Melbourne, and what was seen in Cape Town was then shipped by sea to Rio de Janeiro.

This is where two of the Volvo Ocean Race's associate sponsors, Schenker and the Wallenius

Wilhelmsen shipping line, played a significant role in the success of the event. Schenker, the official logistics supplier of the race, delivered a wide range of services, including air freight, sea freight, land operations, customs clearance, materials-handling equipment, warehousing, spare parts distribution, and event services for all divisions and organisations associated with the race.

Wallenius Wilhelmsen proudly laid claim to having the lead boat into every port visited by the Volvo Ocean Race. Its ships carried a wide array of race support equipment and also transported race yachts *movistar* and *Ericsson* as deck cargo into the next race port after structural damage forced them out of a leg of the race.

Once a shipment landed at the site of a race stopover village each group sent an advance team to begin the assembly process so everything was ready when the yachts, sponsors, media, corporate guests, and the public arrived.

This page, top and bottom: movistar *is lifted aboard the* Wallenius Wilhelmsen MV.

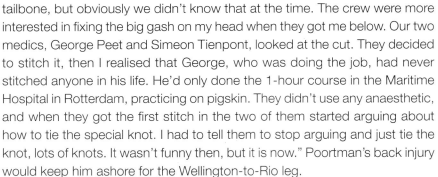

Right: A crewman on movistar *searches for wind in the crucial moments of the race.*
Bottom: Movistar *beats* ABN AMRO ONE *into Wellington by 9 seconds.*

tailbone, but obviously we didn't know that at the time. The crew were more interested in fixing the big gash on my head when they got me below. Our two medics, George Peet and Simeon Tienpont, looked at the cut. They decided to stitch it, then I realised that George, who was doing the job, had never stitched anyone in his life. He'd only done the 1-hour course in the Maritime Hospital in Rotterdam, practicing on pigskin. They didn't use any anaesthetic, and when they got the first stitch in the two of them started arguing about how to tie the special knot. I had to tell them to stop arguing and just tie the knot, lots of knots. It wasn't funny then, but it is now." Poortman's back injury would keep him ashore for the Wellington-to-Rio leg.

Movistar and *ABN AMRO ONE* battled for the lead for the first 19 hours until a slight change in wind direction enabled the Dutch boat to use its reaching headsail with devastating effect. Within a matter of hours, *ABN AMRO ONE* again demonstrated the benefit of having the perfect sail wardrobe as it disappeared over the horizon ahead of its opposition. They wouldn't be seen again until New Zealand came into view.

It appeared that the others would again pick up the crumbs, battling for the minor places on the podium in what was proving to be a physically and mentally challenging leg. Paul Cayard told of the harsh physical demands of gybing in 27–30 knots of wind where the crew had to move 1.5 tonnes of sails, food, and gear to windward after the manoeuvre.

This leg might have been a sprint by Volvo Ocean Race standards, but crews reported that 1,000 nautical miles of it was tough and action-packed—high speeds and solid wind. *ABN AMRO ONE* maintained a 30-plus-nautical-mile lead on approach to Cook Strait between New Zealand's two main islands, but then things began to go pear shaped, as bowman Justin Slattery revealed: "The day before the finish we blasted into Cook Strait, supposedly one of the windiest places in the world, doing 28 knots. Just 30 minutes later we were parked in a millpond: the water was like a glass-topped table.

"*Movistar* came in to the north of us and never stopped. They just sailed around us. The next morning

Amid massive cheering and shouts of encouragement from the crowd, *movistar* squeaked across the line, the winner by the smallest margin ever recorded in the 33-year history of the race—just 9 seconds!

the breeze filled in a little and we set off after them. The sailing that followed over the final 100 nautical miles was about as exciting as you'll get when it comes to one-on-one racing. *Movistar* was ahead of us for about 5 or 6 hours then, during the morning, we picked up quite a nice wind shift up the northern shore and sailed up inside them well enough to just get our bow in front. For the final 6 hours it was just a full-on match race."

When the pair came into the view of the thousands of people lining Wellington's dockfront, *movistar* led by less than a boat length. Amid massive cheering and shouts of encouragement from the crowd, *movistar* squeaked across the line, the winner by the smallest margin ever recorded in the 33-year history of the race—just 9 seconds! It was like the Grand National being won by a nose.

The Black Pearl was another 3 hours back in third, followed by *Brasil 1*, *ABN AMRO TWO*, and *Ericsson*. At the dock *movistar* was found to have the fairing missing around the keel's sliding "bomb doors," forcing skipper Bekking to take a 2-hour penalty for the start of the leg to Rio so repairs could be made.

Top: A nailbiting finish between movistar *and* ABN AMRO ONE.

Right: Movistar, *the happy leg winners.*

Leg 3 Results

Leg Position	Yacht	Elapsed Time	Leg Points	Melbourne In-Port Race Points	Previous Points	Overall Points	Overall Standing
1	movistar	3d 22h 9m 26s	7.0	2.5	15.5	25.0	3
2	ABN AMRO ONE	3d 22h 9m 35s	6.0	3.5	29.0	38.5	1
3	The Black Pearl	4d 0h 59m	5.0	3.0	13.5	21.5	4
4	Brasil 1	4d 3h 12m	4.0	1.5	14.5	20.0	5
5	ABN AMRO TWO	4d 4h 3m	3.0	1.0	24.0	28.0	2
6	Ericsson	6d 0h 57m	2.0	2.0	12.5	16.5	6

"Last time I raced through the Southern Ocean towards Cape Horn we almost died. It was like playing Russian roulette with your life: there was ice everywhere. You could see most of it during the day, but at night it was quite terrifying. You were sailing blind, knowing all the time that there was a good chance you could hit something, but you didn't know what or when. If you said you weren't scared I'd say you had something wrong in your head." Justin Slattery, bowman, *ABN AMRO ONE*

Leg04
Wellingtonto
RiodeJaneiro

For those fortunate enough to be on Queen's Wharf in Wellington late at night on the eve of the start of leg four of the Volvo Ocean Race, the scene was almost surreal—it was utterly opposed to what the Volvo Open 70s and their crews would be subjected to in just a few days. The race yachts sat there in near silence, tethered to the dock like thoroughbred racehorses. Their black, carbon fibre masts, which were highlighted by the warm glow of the nearby city lights, gave barely a hint of stirring, only rocking slightly from side to side on the odd occasion in response to the subtle swell moving across the bay.

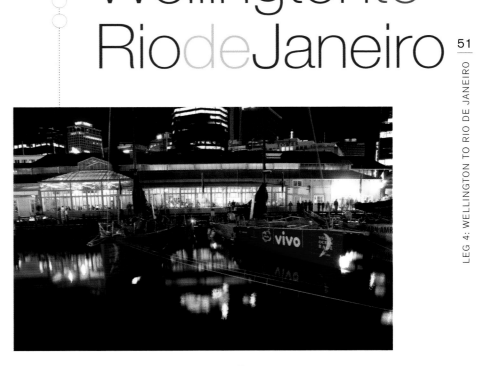

Left: Decks awash
as the crew grind on
board ABN AMRO ONE.

Above: Tethered
like racehorses at
Queen's Wharf.

Scenes from Wellington, clockwise from left: A distracted Tom and Belinda Braidwood try to say a last farewell.

Keeping an even pace with The Black Pearl.

ABN AMRO TWO rolls Ericsson at the start.

Below: New Zealander Scott Beavis, from ABN AMRO TWO, dyes his beard as the New Zealand Fern.

Just hours later the dock was a scene of frenetic activity. Thousands of spectators crammed every vantage point around the wooden wharves, soaking up the excitement. In stark contrast, the tight cluster of crewmembers, their families, and friends were entrenched in last-minute dockside farewells, the air heavy with sentiment. They realised that the most dangerous stage of the race was upon them: the 6,700-nautical-mile stretch across the life-threatening waters of the Southern Ocean to Cape Horn, and on up to Rio de Janeiro.

The most poignant moment, the one that explicitly defined the emotional trauma that this contest can deliver, came as ABN AMRO ONE prepared to depart. Kiwi Mark "Crusty" Christensen sat on the foredeck in the minutes leading up to the dock lines being cast off while his little girls, 7-year-old Madeleine and 3-year-old Bronte, stood with their mother, Janelle, on the dock in front of him. His arm extended through the lifelines and his massive hand enveloped Maddy's. There were smiles and unhurried, idle chatter between two little girls and their father . . . until the realisation came that the yacht was slowly easing away from the dock. His arm extended until he could hold her tiny hand no longer, and simultaneously tears and sobs from the girls ensued: "Daddy, don't go . . . please don't go," Maddy wailed. The big man struggled to cope as the gulf between him and his family widened.

Again the presence of extremely hazardous icefields across the fleet's fastest course to Cape Horn left race organisers with no option but to declare two "ice gates," both around 200 nautical miles long, between Wellington and the Cape. It made sense: the incredible speed of these yachts meant that their closing speed on an obstruction was higher than in any previous race, which in turn meant that the time for taking evasive action would be at an absolute minimum. Dangerous before . . . extremely dangerous now. The first of these gates was established 1,600 nautical miles east of Wellington, while the eastern end of the other was 2,100 nautical miles northwest of Cape Horn. Both were at latitude 48 degrees South.

Wellington turned on brochure weather for the pitstop and the locals took to their first taste of the Volvo Ocean Race with great gusto. When it came time for the restart, there were huge crowds on the shoreline and an impressive fleet of spectator boats. Missing from the immediate action, however, was movistar. She was still at the dock, waiting out the 2-hour time penalty incurred as a consequence of using outside assistance to repair the damage to the hull.

As it would turn out, less than a day out of Wellington movistar rode a strengthening wind to a place within the tight pack, where The Black Pearl and ABN AMRO ONE were leading.

The first tactical challenge came with a decaying tropical cyclone that was destined to cross the fleet's path. Initially it looked like the northerly course of Brasil 1 and ABN AMRO TWO would win out handsomely, but Mike Sanderson's decision to take a dive to the south that lost them

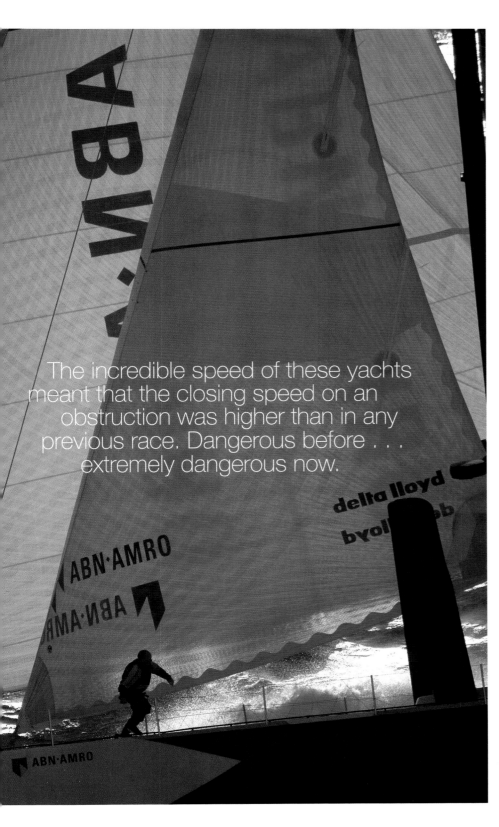

The incredible speed of these yachts meant that the closing speed on an obstruction was higher than in any previous race. Dangerous before . . . extremely dangerous now.

43 nautical miles on the fleet would eventually prove a winner. The Dutch boat led at the first ice gate over *The Black Pearl, movistar, Ericsson, Brasil 1,* and *ABN AMRO TWO,* the latter two dropping to 156 nautical miles and 224 nautical miles behind, respectively, because of an unfavourable and unexpected change in wind direction.

"It seemed ridiculous to be beating our way north in the Southern Ocean to get around the ice gates," said *ABN AMRO ONE's* Justin Slattery. "But then you remind yourself about how dangerous it was last time among the icebergs, and suddenly things are OK."

ABN AMRO ONE kept its pursuers in its wake across both ice gates, then changed course to the southeast, directly towards Cape Horn. Here any thoughts the race crews might have held that they'd escaped the worst of the Southern Ocean weather were quickly extinguished. A punishing gale delivered 50-knot winds and generated towering, powerful, and breaking seas.

"Within 12 hours of putting the bow down towards the Horn we were on our bikes and doing 25 to 30 knots," Slattery reported. "We maintained the pace all the way to the corner and did 4 consecutive days of 500-plus miles. It was awesome sailing—unheard of in monohull racing."

For Mike Sanderson this was the stage of the race where *ABN AMRO ONE* proved just how great a yacht she is. "The design of the boat is aggressively oriented towards reaching. She's a very fat boat with a high prismatic coefficient, a feature that meant that down south, running dead downwind in big waves, it was going to be very hard work for us; on-the-

Left: Checking the staysail on board ABN AMRO ONE.
Top: Daybreak on movistar.
Bottom: Putting up with the cold, bowman Justin Slattery from ABN AMRO ONE looks miserable.

53

When the wind was really howling and the seas at their worst, the crews braced for the toughest 24 hours of the 17,000 nautical miles covered so far. Some waves were cresting at 20 metres.

From left: Ericsson *heads back into the Southern Ocean.*

The sun rises over the bow of Brasil 1.

Waves crash across Brasil 1 *as they near Cape Horn.*

edge sailing on a boat that would not be forgiving. So for us to be able to put the hammer down during this gale, score the highest 6-hour run on the leg, and lead through the scoring gate at Cape Horn . . . that was the 'biggy.'"

Still, it was dangerous sailing, especially at night, as the *Ericsson* crew was quick to learn. They were on a charge in 25 knots of wind with a full mainsail and their largest spinnaker—500 square metres—powering them at 20+ knots. First came a massive broach—a wipeout—then, after recovering from that, an even worse situation, a "Chinese gybe." The yacht went out of control again, screamed off course to leeward, the sails went aback, and *Ericsson* was flattened: pinned on its side with the mast almost in the water. The sails were flogging wildly and the entire yacht shuddered under the pressure while it tried to right itself. Soon after, an exhausted Neal McDonald gave a graphic account of the drama by radio: "Pitch black . . . and terrifying. There's no other way of putting it. Anybody who has done a Chinese gybe in broad daylight would know the ferocity and the scare that is involved: it really is very violent. I was below deck and there the whole world was upside down: you're walking on people in their bunks rather than on the floor. It really is a very peculiar sensation. My first thought was for the four guys on deck. I stuck my head out of the hatch—you know you're not going to see anything—so I was listening for four voices. I've got no idea what I was expecting, and those are the moments I really don't want to repeat: I had no

"My first thought was for the four guys on deck. I stuck my head out of the hatch—you know you're not going to see anything—so I was listening for four voices. I had no idea if they'd be there, or still be alive."
Neal McDonald, skipper, *Ericsson*

idea if they'd be there, or still be alive. It really was quite terrifying . . . those first few seconds when I stuck my head out of the hatch waiting to hear the guys say 'Yeah, I'm all right. I'm here.'"

When the wind was really howling and the seas at their worst, the crews braced for the toughest 24 hours of the 17,000 nautical miles covered so far. Some waves were cresting at 20 metres, the fog made the atmosphere a miserable grey colour, the water temperature was getting close to 5 degrees Celsius, and it was getting colder by the hour. Still, no one was ready to back off, as was evident by the fact that both *The Black Pearl* and *movistar* were starting to achieve average speeds that were threatening *ABN AMRO TWO's* world-record, 24-hour run of 563 nautical

Clockwise from left: Andrew Lewis looks out towards the sunrise from ABN AMRO TWO.
ABN AMRO TWO *heads south.*
The crew hold tightly onto movistar.

miles. It was wild and very wet racing, especially for the crewmembers faced with working in "frontier land"—up on the foredeck. In this weather it's like being a mountain climber . . . dangling on a sheer rockface where your umbilical cord, the only thing between life and death, is the thin strop on your safety harness. Justin Slattery told of the experience: "There are times when you have to go forward and you just know that the bow is going to go in: spear through the wave that's ahead. It's not too bad when you're doing 20 knots, but even then you don't rely solely on your harness. When you know that the moment is coming you just get down and hug the deck and hold on as hard as you can to anything you can find. It's a different story when you're up there and the yacht's doing between 35 and 40 knots. There's no way you're going to physically be able to hang on in a nosedive . . . suddenly you're completely under water, green water that's probably a metre over your head, and you go tumbling aft. You can feel different parts of the boat hitting your body as you go, and you're trying to figure out where you are so you might be able to grab onto something. It might be the lifelines brushing past you, or the daggerboard, the mast, or rigging: you're still under water and just don't know where you are while all the time waiting for impact. Then you're wondering if you have gone past it

Guillermo Altadill defines sailing in the Southern Ocean: This was the leg I was most looking forward to. It was the longest and most adventurous one of the race. We would be sailing against the elements; strong conditions, big waves, freezing cold weather. This was also the leg where we round Cape Horn, and you can't say you have sailed around the world unless you have rounded the Horn. For me it would be my sixth time!

THE CONTEST

When I saw the faces of the crew during my watch, someone shouted, 'don't look back, Guillermo!' I realised that the big waves we'd had during the last few hours, which had made us surf at 30 knots, had become even bigger. They had exceeded the limits between fun and danger.

When I did decide to look back to satisfy my curiosity, I saw what only nature is able to create: millions of tonnes of water moving at considerable speed. Really, I won't forget this rounding of Cape Horn, and I'll remember a concrete wave with my name on it—like an epitaph on a headstone in a cemetery.

I've been asked many times if I'd ever been scared during the round-the-world races I'd done before. The answer wasn't really easy, because it's hard to be scared while competing: competition and fear are incompatible things, or at least, that's what I thought.

From here on I'll have a more concrete answer. During my sixth rounding of Cape Horn I was really scared. And I think that anyone who had been in my place on that day, with winds of 50 knots and waves like I'd never seen, would also have been scared. I now understand the old stories about helmsmen not being allowed to look back in hard swell conditions. The reason is evident: if he saw what was coming behind he would be so scared that he would become a real danger for the whole crew.

The reason for the formation of the massive Cape Horn waves is that the sea bottom goes suddenly from being 4,000 metres deep to a depth of just 70 metres, creating an enormous step where the Southern Ocean's big waves become huge holes that can simply gobble up a considerable-sized yacht. This remote spot of Southern Patagonia has registered the highest number of yacht losses in history. The Horn's storms are well known since ancient times.

For several hours, our crew on *Ericsson* gave up competing and just tried to survive and round the legendary Horn out of danger. I suffered 2 weeks of cold, tiredness, and tension competing in one of the more inhospitable places of the world: the Southern Ocean. If I had to define what hell is like, I could describe it as a night sailing in these waters in rough seas.

Top: Duck! Heavy spray pounds Brasil 1.

Bottom: Go hoist . . . the bowman signals with his hand as he is silhoutted agaist the rising sun, working on the foredeck of Ericsson.

"When I did look back to satisfy my curiosity, I saw what only nature is able to create: millions of tonnes of water moving at considerable speed."
Guillermo Altadill, crewmember, *Ericsson*

all. There's enormous relief when you finally do have impact: you know then that you're still on the boat and not dangling over the side on your safety harness, being dragged along at 35 knots."

For the newcomers to round-the-world racing, this was the most testing time. Aboard *Ericsson* the big Kiwi race veteran, Richard Mason, brought a reality check to those who were sitting on deck in the middle of a miserable, storm-laden night declaring how exhausted they were: "You guys don't know what being tired is," he bellowed. "This is easy. Being tired is when you've got two young kids at home that keep you up all night."

The yachts continued on their stunning charge towards Cape Horn. *ABN AMRO ONE* maintained its lead, but not far astern the boys on *movistar* had the world 24-hour record in their sights and were driving hard. It was around 3 am and they were achieving an average well over 20 knots, delicately balanced on a tightrope in the grip of the Southern Ocean storm. Suddenly a dreaded, panic-laden call bellowed from the blacked-out cabin below. "We are sinking! Everybody up! Slow the boat down, the water is coming in very fast! And close the watertight hatches."

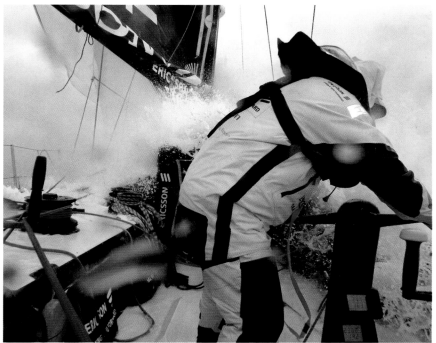

Clockwise from left: Guillermo Altadill at the helm of Ericsson. *Brasil 1 nears Cape Horn. Waves breaking over* Ericsson.

"When you're up there and the yacht's doing between 35 and 40 knots, there's no way you're going to physically be able to hang on in a nosedive . . . suddenly you're completely under water, green water that's probably a metre over your head, and you go tumbling aft. There's enormous relief when you find that you're still on the boat and not dangling over the side on your safety harness, being dragged along at 35 knots." Justin Slattery, bowman, *ABN AMRO ONE*

Crewman grinding as waves wash over the decks of ABN AMRO ONE.

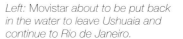

Left: Movistar *about to be put back in the water to leave Ushuaia and continue to Rio de Janeiro.*

Right: Pepe Ribes *trimming and Stu Bannatyne at the helm as the sun rises on board* movistar.

Movistar's *skipper Bouwe Bekking holds a crew meeting in Ushuaia.*

Suddenly a dreaded, panic-laden call bellowed from the blacked-out cabin below. "We are sinking! Everybody up! Slow the boat down, the water is coming in very fast! And close the watertight hatches."

From that instant the fight was on to save the yacht. Navigator Andrew Cape immediately informed race headquarters of *movistar's* plight and requested that yachts directly behind them, *Brasil 1* and *Ericsson*, be alerted in case they were needed for assistance, possibly even a rescue. Simultaneously, those on deck lowered the sails to slow the boat, while Peter "Spike" Doriean prepared the emergency safety equipment in the cockpit and readied the life rafts in case the call was to "abandon ship."

The source of the problem was quickly discovered. The "bomb doors" around the keel had failed, causing the top to explode off the watertight keel box. Near freezing water was bursting into the main cabin as though a massive water pipe had broken.

Chris Nicholson takes up the story: "When I jumped out of my bunk into near waist-deep water, I knew that we had to get the pumps going immediately. But with the electrics already flooded, there was no way they were going to start. I knew there was only one thing to do—wire the pumps

directly to the battery terminals so they would start and not stop running. The batteries were, by then, under water in watertight bags, so each time I dived to find the terminals and try to secure the cables to them, I was saying to myself, 'oh dear, I know what's coming here . . . a bloody great whack.' There were a few arcs and sparks and plenty of bad words from me each time I copped a boot."

Nicholson took the 24-volt jolt through his body some 20 times before he finally succeeded and the pumps started. At that moment the water level in the cabin was only 50 centimetres from where the yacht would have had to be abandoned. For his efforts Nicholson received the Musto Seamanship Award at the leg four trophy presentation in Rio.

It was day 12 of the leg, and while *movistar* headed for Ushuaia, Argentina, for repairs, *ABN AMRO ONE* reached latitude 55° 58' 28" South and surged past the craggy, bleak, leviathan cliffs of Cape Horn, taking maximum points at the scoring gate in doing so. It was an

Clockwise from left: Heavy
weather for Brasil 1.

The Brasil 1 crew celebrate
rounding Cape Horn.

Tim Powell at the helm as
a rainbow forms on the
horizon behind Ericsson.

"I looked up to the top of the mast and couldn't
believe what I was seeing – it was on fire! We
were in the heaviest rain you've ever seen and
there were flames literally flaring at the top of
the rig." Steve Hayles, navigator, Ericsson

achievement that carried special meaning for the crew of the Dutch entry. Mike Sanderson reminded everyone that the world's most famous and notorious cape was first conquered by a Dutchman: "In 1616 the explorer Willem Corneliszoon Schouten, who was born in the Dutch city of Hoorn, braved furious storms as he rounded the southernmost tip of South America. He named it Kaap Hoorn (Cape Horn) in honour of his hometown."

The Black Pearl was second past the Horn and through the gate ahead of Brasil 1, ABN AMRO TWO, and Ericsson, which was once again struggling for speed. The yachts in the latter part of the fleet experienced legendary Cape Horn weather—a wind gusting from behind at up to 50 knots and mountainous seas.

Amazingly, only a short distance from the point where they left the Southern Ocean, entered the Atlantic, and turned north towards Rio, they were almost becalmed. It was symptomatic of what lay ahead—tense, tactical, and primarily light-weather sailing all the way to Rio de Janeiro, 2,000 miles away. The fleet compressed, from more than 200 nautical miles between first and last place, to a span of less than 50 nautical miles.

The one drama on the passage north came during a turbulent thunderstorm when Ericsson was struck by a bolt of lightning that set their mast on fire and blew out most of their electronics. "About 3 days out of Rio we hooked into a cold front coming off the South American coast," said Steve Hayles. "It was a typical system for the region—loads of rain and hail,

Left: Skipper Paul Cayard at the helm, silhouetted against the setting sun on board The Black Pearl.

Right: The ABN AMRO ONE *crew celebrate another win with a local Samba dancer.*

Below: Brasil 1 skipper Torben Grael faces the media after finishing fourth.

a wind that would go from calm to 35 knots very quickly, and just as quickly change to the opposite direction. Next thing the lightning started all around us, and suddenly we were hit. The noise was phenomenal, just the most amazing cracking sound, and we knew the boat had been hit. It wasn't quite enough to knock people on their backsides, but it wasn't far off. I looked up to the top of the mast and couldn't believe what I was seeing—it was on fire! We were in the heaviest rain you've ever seen and there were flames literally flaring at the top of the rig. Fortunately everyone was safe and the fire went out, but most of the electrics and computers were blown out."

It was a game of snakes and ladders all the way from Cape Horn to the finish; sometimes you gained, other times you lost. Little more than 100 nautical miles from Rio, Torben Grael had sailed *Brasil 1* into second place, only to slide back to fourth at the finish. *ABN AMRO ONE* maintained an advantage over *The Black Pearl* through to the line to take first place while the young team on *ABN AMRO TWO* stole third spot on the podium right at the death. *Ericsson* came home a disappointing fifth, and to no one's surprise, a crew reshuffle and new skipper was announced soon after.

Leg 4 Results

Leg Position	Yacht	Elapsed Time	Leg Points	Cape Horn Scoring Gate Points	Previous Points	Overall Points	Overall Standing
1	ABN AMRO ONE	20d 1h 48m	7.0	3.5	38.5	49.0	1
2	The Black Pearl	20d 5h 36m	6.0	3.0	21.5	30.5	3
3	ABN AMRO TWO	20d 6h 6m	5.0	2.0	28.0	35.0	2
4	Brasil 1	20d 6h 25m	4.0	2.5	20.0	26.5	5
5	Ericsson	20d 17h 42m	3.0	1.5	16.5	21.0	6
6	movistar	25d 14h 41m	2.0	1.0	25.0	28.0	4

"Jerry Kirby had only just told us nothing ever happened in the Bermuda Triangle when hell broke loose. We suddenly lost all power on the yacht, the keel wouldn't cant and we were in the middle of a howling rainstorm. While we tried to get things sorted all you could hear was the guys shouting, 'No Bermuda Triangle, huh? Good on you Jerry. Thanks for putting a hex on us.'"
Anthony Merrington, crewmember, *The Black Pearl*

"Game On" was the theory held by many crews and Volvo Ocean Race observers at the start of leg five from Rio de Janeiro to Baltimore. This was the time when all boats would be finely tuned, bullet-proof, and in prime condition to challenge the clear-cut superiority shown so far by Mike Sanderson's *ABN AMRO ONE.*

The theory was reinforced by a belief that "Black Betty" would be hamstrung in the anticipated lighter conditions, and with well over half of the total race points still up for grabs, the end result in Göteborg was far from a foregone conclusion.

ABN AMRO ONE exerted her authority in the in-port race, staged

Leg05
RiodeJaneiro
toBaltimore

Left: Looking for a comeback, ABN AMRO TWO *sails upright and fast.*

Above: Movistar *creeps up the Chesapeake Bay towards Baltimore to take second place.*

Clockwise from top:
André Fonseca, trimmer and
helmsman of Brasil 1, before leaving the
dock for the in-port race on Guanabara
Bay, Rio de Janeiro, Brazil.
Justin Clougher looks for wind in
the in-port race.
The Rio in-port race is a light wind affair.

on Rio's Guanabara Bay, delivering enthusiastic supporters a wire-to-wire win over *movistar,* while *Ericsson* saw the podium for the first time since Sanxenxo by filling a third. Local hero Torben Grael was expected to excel on his home waters with *Brasil 1*, but as a consequence of either stage fright or the pressure of the moment, he first broke the start and was recalled, then incurred a 360-degree penalty turn for a rule breach near the first mark.

While April Fool's Day jokes had people believe Paul Cayard had been sacked from *The Black Pearl,* and that Mike Sanderson enjoyed the sumptuous comfort of a five-star private cabin aboard "Black Betty," the only real change came aboard *Ericsson.* John Kostecki was put in harness as skipper while Neal McDonald remained aboard as a watch captain.

Some 20,000 people were either on the water or along the shoreline to farewell the yachts under a canopy of thin, high clouds on a sultry Rio day. With a light onshore breeze fanning across the bay, *Ericsson* led away from the line, much to the pleasure of the yacht's godmother, Her Royal Highness Crown Princess Victoria of Sweden, who had spent more than a week in Rio to support the team, and was watching from a spectator boat. But fluky wind conditions around the entrance of the bay helped *The Black Pearl* cruise to the front and lead at the turning mark positioned off the famous Copacabana Beach. It was a disappointing exit for *ABN AMRO ONE*. A halyard lock failed and sent the yacht's headsail fluttering to the deck soon after the

The 5,000-nautical-mile course from Rio de Janeiro to Baltimore could be compared with a championship golf course. The fairways were the trade winds the fleet would experience either side of the equator; the sand traps were the Doldrums; the rough could well be found off the coast of Florida and northwards; and the undulating, hard-to-read, very tricky green was the massive expanse of water making up Chesapeake Bay.

start, and as a result she reached the turn in last place, 18 minutes astern of the leader.

But that deficit was quickly erased. The relatively light reaching conditions on the first night were tailor-made for the black boat and within 24 hours she was, not surprisingly, at the head of the pack. Sanderson's race plan was to sail conservatively during the early stages and stay with the majority of the fleet, but it would prove expensive. Bouwe Bekking guided *movistar* on a course inshore of the others and opened up a healthy advantage inside 2 days of leaving Rio, quickly moving from 22 miles astern of the leader, to 25 nautical miles ahead.

Mother Nature had bowled an unseen problem that cost them dearly on the first night: "It was a nightmare," Bekking said. "We parked without wind under a cloud we could do nothing about and missed the train ride north—

the others were gone . . . 22 nautical miles ahead in no time. We also had something wrapped around the keel so we had to stop and do a 'back-down' to get rid of that. We always wanted to be inside the fleet and close to shore, but because of our experience coming out of Cape Town, where we lost everything by separating too far, we were conservative this time. In hindsight, I think that anyone who was game enough to go to the extreme and sail just 10 nautical miles off the coast would have very quickly been 200 nautical miles ahead. There was more pressure in there."

All competitors went through numerous rounds of Russian roulette with the clouds in this tropical region: if you were able to get your yacht positioned perfectly on the favoured side of a cloud sweeping across the course then you got breeze. If you got it wrong then you

Top: Movistar *rounds the first mark in the in-port race.*
Below: Keeping cool on Brasil 1.

missed the ride. Because of this, positions rapidly changed in an almost ridiculous fashion. *ABN AMRO ONE* crashed from fourth (behind *movistar*, *The Black Pearl,* and *ABN AMRO TWO)*, to last place, only to get some favourable breeze and climb back to fourth.

Being a navigator in a race like this is often a thankless and extremely tiring task. Recognising that, Bekking took time out to salute Andrew Cape: "I have sailed in plenty of ocean races, and I have to admit that most of the navigators I have sailed with are a special breed. Capey is, in that sense, no exception. Capey is fantastic at his job: skilled with computers, making good calls, positive and very funny.

If you were able to get your yacht positioned perfectly on the favoured side of a cloud sweeping across the course then you got breeze. If you got it wrong then you missed the ride.

"I love to peek out of my bunk when Capey is at work. Sometimes he goes without sleep for 24 hours. Like tonight for example. He was working on some programme, headset on and music on full tilt, tapping continuously on the keyboard. But then, all of a sudden, sleep had the winning hand. His head started rolling and rocking a couple times, but he kept pushing the key tabs. Then, all of a sudden, his head rocked forward and crashed with a loud bang, onto the nav station. I nearly rolled out of my bunk with laughter. He was sound asleep while lying in an impossible position."

By the time the scoring gate at the island of Fernando de Noronha was reached—6 days and 1,000 nautical miles from Rio—the recovery by Sanderson's team was amazingly close to complete. They trailed *movistar* by just 1 minute 25 seconds, but only minutes later the Dutch boat showed superior surfing ability under its powerful reaching spinnaker and surged into the lead—a lead that would be maintained to Chesapeake Bay. Bekking was impressed: "I have to admit, even though I hated this happening to us, it was a pretty awesome sight when they rolled over the top of us with a boat length in between. Raw power!"

Soon the fleet was riding the refreshing trade winds through the tropics towards the equator, enjoying champagne sailing. But it wasn't without incident, as Paul Cayard revealed: "Last night we were attacked by flying fish. One centre-punched Craig Satterthwaite right between the eyes and

Changing the skipper's mind: *Brunel*'s navigator, Will Oxley, drew international media interest to the Volvo Ocean Race with this piece, written after *Brunel* rejoined the fleet in Baltimore.

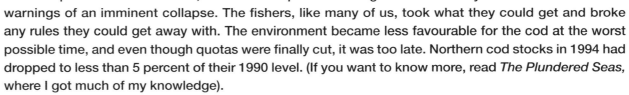

In my other life I am a marine scientist and I seem to lie to the left of the general population in terms of my environmental views. When we are racing up the coast of Australia for example, I am commenting on how great it is that so much of the area is national park while Grant (Grant Wharington) and GT (Graeme Taylor) are salivating over what a great site an undisturbed beach would be for a development. OK, so having declared my biases, I'd like to tell you a story.

The Grand Banks off the coast of North America is famous for 'The Perfect Storm' but more importantly, one of the worst ever collapses of a fish stock: the cod. The finger cannot be pointed at any one group for this collapse. Instead it is a classic case of a 'Tragedy of the Commons.'

The biologists overestimated the stock size, and then, under pressure from the fishers, the managers set fish quotas even higher than suggested by the biologist's wrong figures. Increasingly effective trawlers caught more and more fish. The politicians didn't listen, or lacked the political strength to act on early warnings of an imminent collapse. The fishers, like many of us, took what they could get and broke any rules they could get away with. The environment became less favourable for the cod at the worst possible time, and even though quotas were finally cut, it was too late. Northern cod stocks in 1994 had dropped to less than 5 percent of their 1990 level. (If you want to know more, read *The Plundered Seas*, where I got much of my knowledge).

We are in danger of repeating this story around the world, particularly with stocks of the orange roughy, a very popular table fish. Until about 30 years ago they lived below depths at which we were able to fish (500 fathoms or more), then, over the last 20 years, we have set about decimating the stocks all over the world to supply the demand for these fish. If we do not do something about it then the orange roughy will go the same way of the cod.

I've been doing my bit in rather unconventional ways. Matt (Matt Humphries), GT, and I were sitting down to dinner at a restaurant in Mornington, Australia, late one night during the refit of *Brunel* and Matt ordered the orange roughy. I said, 'You can't eat that fish: it is becoming an endangered species, and by the way, it is probably quite old!'

'How old?' asked Matt, not worrying about the first part of my statement.

Dragging out memories of some fisheries course, I guessed that it was probably 75 years old!

'Yuk' said Matt, 'I'm not eating anything that's older than my grandmother,' and changed his order.

It created quite a laugh and has been an on-going joke. After the meal I checked up on the orange roughy and the oldest one has been recorded as 150 years old! That has got to be enough to stop you eating them.

The statue of Christ looks down upon ABN AMRO TWO *as she sails past Sugarloaf Mountain.*

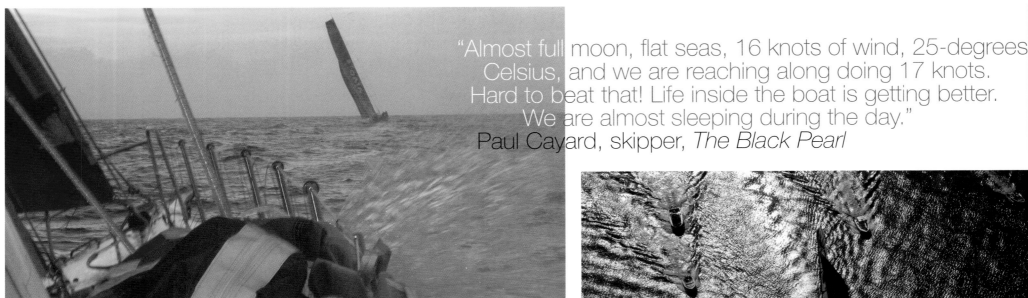

"Almost full moon, flat seas, 16 knots of wind, 25-degrees Celsius, and we are reaching along doing 17 knots. Hard to beat that! Life inside the boat is getting better. We are almost sleeping during the day."
Paul Cayard, skipper, *The Black Pearl*

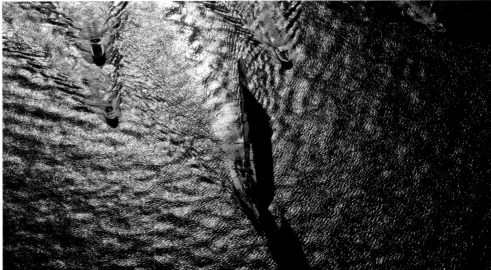

Top: Brasil 1 *pulls away from* The Black Pearl.

Right: Movistar *supported by friends as she glides through the water on the way to the finish.*

knocked him down. These little rockets are attracted to the lights on our instruments at night and come flying at the boat. They are very hard-headed so they hurt when they hit you, sometimes at speeds up to 20 knots."

Fortunately on this leg the usually wide, windless void that makes up the Doldrums near the equator was again almost non-existent and the fleet made a rapid, procession-like exit. The fleet was spread out over 175 nautical miles with *ABN AMRO ONE* leading *movistar, The Black Pearl, Brasil 1, Ericsson,* and *ABN AMRO TWO*. Fast trade-wind sailing along the outskirts of the Caribbean was to follow before entering the "mystery zone," 600 nautical miles east of Florida: the Bermuda Triangle.

This is where strange things are said to happen, but *The Black Pearl* crewman Jerry Kirby was quick to declare it was all bunkum . . . then hell

broke loose. Suddenly the yacht lost all electrical power, the keel wouldn't cant, and they were in the middle of a howling rainstorm.

Sebastien Josse's team aboard *ABN AMRO TWO* would later experience a very different problem below deck that came during a sail change. As the spinnakers were being dragged aft in the cabin, a wayward boot resulted in the contents of one of the fire extinguishers exploding through the interior. Suddenly there were crewmembers bursting through the hatch and into the cockpit, gasping for air and looking like they were covered in flour.

The Gulf Stream delivered the usual conveyor-belt ride north, but it was far from pleasant sailing, reaching along in a 25-knot wind and nasty head sea. For Torben Grael's team on *Brasil 1* the conditions were so wide ranging that in a matter of hours they'd tried all but two of the entire wardrobe of sails they carried.

Memories of their 9-second loss to *movistar* going into Wellington, after holding a 35-mile lead 100 nautical miles out, haunted the *ABN AMRO ONE* team as they entered Chesapeake Bay for the final stretch to Baltimore.

Leg 5 Results

Leg Position	Yacht	Elapsed Time	Leg Points	Rio In-Port Race Points	Rio Scoring Gate Points	Previous Points	Overall Points	Overall Standing
1	ABN AMRO ONE	15d 2h 47m	7.0	3.5	3.0	49.0	62.5	1
2	movistar	15d 8h 4m	6.0	3.0	3.5	28.0	40.5	2
3	The Black Pearl	15d 19h 12m	5.0	1.0	2.5	30.5	39.0	4
4	Brasil 1	15d 21h 11m	4.0	2.0	1.5	26.5	34.0	5
5	Ericsson	15d 21h 23m	3.0	2.5	2.0	21.0	28.5	6
6	ABN AMRO TWO	15d 22h 31m	2.0	1.5	1.0	35.0	39.5	3

Even after having taken out four of the five ocean legs, and three of the four in-port races, **Mike Sanderson** was in a state of denial: "I'm not saying we've won it. We still need more points to win this race. We'll come last on the next leg between here and New York if we get light airs. Our Achilles Heel will be the short legs like that one."

It was déjà vu—the relative distance from the finish and between the two yachts was about the same again, and conditions ahead were looking very light. Things were going well for the leader until, with the finish line in sight, the breeze died and the tide turned against them. For only the third time in his long career, Sanderson had to call on the anchor to be dropped to stop the loss. Eventually the breeze returned and after 15 days of racing *ABN AMRO ONE* was the victor by more than 5 hours over *movistar*, with *The Black Pearl* third. During one of the most spectacular offshore thunderstorms many sailors had ever seen, *Ericsson* lost fourth place when flattened by a 50-knot squall and subsequently trailed *Brasil 1* home by just 12 minutes. *ABN AMRO TWO* had to survive a near dismasting on approach to Chesapeake Bay before finishing sixth.

Sanderson was, however, pleased to state that the speed of his yacht while sailing north from Rio must have been demoralising for the opposition: "I think some crews are going to come in and talk about the speed of 'Black Betty.' Few people realise that this was the leg our boat was designed for. It was power-reaching most of the way and we had to sail past just about everyone at some stage, often only a few metres away. Previously it's been easy to justify a loss if you didn't see the opposition pass you. You could say, 'Oh, they had better breeze,' or 'they had more wind,' but when you actually see someone sail past you, then it's a case of 'Well, okay, they're going faster than we are.' On this leg it was pretty tough on the others to watch us go past. There is now no argument that we were dominant."

This page, left: Ericsson hard on the wind in the closing stages of the leg.

Top: The Black Pearl on the wind in the Chesapeake Bay nearing the finish line.

"I've just found the meanest wild bull of a boat I've ever sailed. This thing doesn't want to be ridden. In more than 30 years of offshore racing I've never experienced a more violent motion when sailing upwind."
Jerry Kirby, bowman, *The Black Pearl*

Annapolis, on the western shore of the mighty Chesapeake Bay, lived up to its reputation as the "Sailing Capital of the USA" when 35,000 spectators took to the water aboard 3,500 boats to bid farewell to the Volvo Ocean Race fleet at the start of leg six, a 400-nautical-mile coastal dash to New York.

The stopover had been an enormously successful joint venture between the vibrant city of Baltimore and nearby Annapolis, a charming waterfront centre that is steeped in American political and maritime history.

In Baltimore nearly 350,000 people experienced the waterfront festival that was presented in celebration of the Volvo Ocean Race, and in Annapolis people

Leg06
Annapolis
toNew York

Left: Tightly packed on the start line for leg six, to the east of Thomas Point off Annapolis.

Above: The fleet is blessed by The Reverend Mamie Alethia Williams before making their way out to the starting line.

In Annapolis, teams had to decide what sails and equipment needed to be on board to get them to New York and then across the Atlantic to Portsmouth.

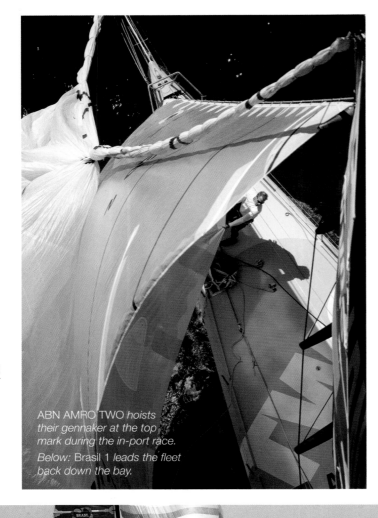

ABN AMRO TWO *hoists their gennaker at the top mark during the in-port race.*

Below: Brasil 1 *leads the fleet back down the bay.*

Right: Chesapeake Bay, packed with spectator boats watching the start of leg six.
Below: Determined for a good result, the Ericsson *crew give it their best.*

queued throughout the day to get a glimpse of the world's fastest offshore racing yachts.

One week before the re-start, thousands of enthusiastic spectators had boarded hundreds of boats to watch yet another entertaining in-port race. An 8-knot breeze that barely ruffled the surface of the bay shaped the contest as one where the fat ladies, in the form of both ABN AMRO entries and the much-modified Australian boat, renamed for the third time and now called *Brunel*, would struggle to sing. It would prove to be a benefit for the narrower Bruce Farr designs. It was a seesawing affair up front with a strong current and wind shifts dealing the cards. *The Black Pearl* led early, much to the delight of the special guest, the newly crowned Miss USA, Tara Elizabeth Conner of Kentucky. But the eventual masters of the day were aboard *movistar*. Back in Baltimore, when the champagne exploded into the air, Bouwe Bekking's team stood atop the podium. Second place went to an ecstatic *Brasil 1* crew while *The Black Pearl* took third.

The following week was a hectic one for the crews and their shore teams: it was a double whammy. As well as having to get their yachts converted from inshore racing mode to a long-distance offshore configuration, they had to prepare for the next two legs as if they were one. With New York a pitstop, special rules were in place. No extra equipment could go on board in New York and there could be no outside assistance to repair breakages. It meant that in Annapolis, teams had to decide what sails and equipment needed to be on board to get them to New York and then across the Atlantic to Portsmouth.

Grant Wharington's *Brunel* was holding considerable attention, having returned to the fray after undergoing rapid and extensive modifications in Melbourne. She now looked very much a modern Volvo Open 70 with twin retractable dagger boards, a ballast bulb shaped more like a torpedo than a house brick, larger rudders, and rig refinements. There was one other significant change in the fleet for this next leg: one of manpower. Neal McDonald was back as skipper of *Ericsson* and Mark Rudiger, who navigated *EF Language* to victory 8 years earlier, replaced Steve Hayles. Two other sailors of note had also stepped aboard, American Ken Read and Australia's Ian "Barney" Walker.

Come the start of the leg to New York, *ABN AMRO ONE's* skipper, Mike Sanderson, found himself haunted by light winds once more. The 10–12 knots that would convert his light-weather plodder into a virtually unbeatable thoroughbred weren't expected to eventuate until near the entrance to the Chesapeake, more than 100 nautical miles away. It meant that by then, in those light conditions Black Betty and the two other "big" boats could be an irrecoverable distance behind the race leaders, no matter what weather came for the remaining 300 nautical miles. It seemed Sanderson's declaration in Baltimore after the leg from Rio, that the race was still far from won, was ringing true.

His worst fears were confirmed when a lethargic-looking *ABN AMRO ONE* struggled for speed, while Torben Grael's *Brasil 1* slid away under spinnaker towards the entrance of the Chesapeake with the other Farr boats in hot pursuit. The weather forecast was for plenty of wind offshore, but that was a long way off, and Black Betty could only wait. *ABN AMRO TWO* and *Brunel* were also struggling. The news wasn't good aboard *movistar* either.

While their speed was fine they suffered a massive failure in the winch drive system only minutes into the race. Their two main winches were not working so every major sail-trimming manoeuvre for the rest of the leg would be painstakingly slow.

White water floods over the bow of ABN AMRO TWO *as she heads for Baltimore.*

Belinda Braidwood, the school mistress of the high seas

When a world-class sailor with a young family cannot resist the temptation of the Volvo Ocean Race and takes to the high seas for 8 months, it can be exceptionally tough on his wife and children. Previously there were two options for the family: see dad briefly on the odd occasion when he could fly home during a stopover, or pack up and travel with him.

While the latter scenario held considerable merit because it kept the family unit intact, it also had its problems, especially when it came to schooling for the children . . . until 31-year-old Australian schoolteacher Belinda Braidwood stepped in.

She was aware that in the 1997–98 race the mothers of young children travelling from port to port were "going crazy trying to home-school their kids." So, when her husband Tom was chosen as a crewmember for *SEB* in the 2001–02 Volvo Ocean Race she came up with a solution and took it to *SEB's* skipper, Gurra Krantz: "I told him about the problem the mothers were facing and offered a solution— I would establish a school during each stopover to help the children, and the mothers. Gurra had a 6-year-old daughter and he thought it was a great idea. *SEB* agreed to sponsor the school and allocated an area in their pavilion to be the classroom. Children from all teams were welcome and it turned out to be a huge success.

In fact the "on the road" school became such an important ingredient of that edition of the Volvo Ocean Race, it was deemed to be essential for the 2005–06 event.

Top left: Belinda Braidwood with pre-school children.

Top right: Belinda Braidwood (left) and Bryony Percy (right), teachers of Volvo Ocean Race School, with pupils visiting the Volvo Open 70s.

"The Volvo Ocean Race management people called me before the start of this race, even before Tommy was selected to crew on *Ericsson*, and said they'd like to do the school again," Belinda explained. "I told Tom I thought it would be great to do it, and that he could come along as the school's librarian if he didn't get a ride on a yacht. That didn't impress him.

"Obviously the kids come from all different countries. Those at primary school stage, between the ages of 5 and 12, are asked to bring maths and English correspondence work with them so we can work through it with them.

"The other work that we do is based around the race and learning about the countries we visit. The children benefit enormously from the cultural experiences in those countries. We also try to learn as much as we can about the competing yachts and the countries they represent. We invite sailors and shore team members into the classroom so the children can interview them."

Belinda was impressed by how the non-English-speaking children adapted. "It's amazing how quickly children from different countries can communicate and learn a new language. Certainly playing together helps a lot towards that. We have two little French girls and another from Denmark who could read and speak English perfectly before the race was half complete."

Volvo Ocean Race management also took the opportunity to establish a section for pre-school children, between 3 and 5 years old, during the 2005–06 race.

With 15 children in the primary school and another 18 in the pre-school, Belinda had to call in help from other mothers and partners who had school-teaching backgrounds. Fortunately there were plenty of takers.

And Belinda already has one certain enrollment for the next race. She and Tom were expecting their first child to be born soon after the completion of the 2005–06 contest.

Justin Clougher perches in the spreaders of The Black Pearl.

THE CONTEST

"I cannot help thinking there must be an easier way to get to New York!"
Simon Fisher, navigator, *ABN AMRO TWO*

ABN AMRO ONE navigator Stan Honey made the first big contribution to their comeback by plotting a course that cut a corner near the entrance to the bay, a manoeuvre that claimed back one precious mile. Then, as the wind began to build, came an "awesome sail change." In just 18 minutes the crew managed to lower the headsail they were using, set a temporary headsail, set a new large headsail, get rid of the temporary sail, and reef the mainsail to a more manageable size. *ABN AMRO ONE* was now back in the hunt and in her element. As one rival sailor would say later in New York "we could only wave them through."

Soon after the weather front crossed the fleet, ferocious upwind conditions were prevailing. Some yachts experienced gusts to 50 knots and the seas were torturous. In these conditions small problems could quickly compound into large ones, as *ABN AMRO TWO* navigator Simon Fisher conveyed: "I cannot help thinking there must be an easier way to get to

From left: First to finish. ABN AMRO ONE *passes the Statue of Liberty.*
The Statue of Liberty welcomes Brunel *as they finish in New York.*

New York! So far on leg six we have seen everything from calms to 55-knot squalls and we have only been on the water a little over 24 hours! We have spent the majority of our time pounding upwind, getting tossed around like pancakes as we struggle to hold on to the boat as she bucks and rears over the waves. The rain is coming across the deck horizontally as are the waves.

"We have been dogged by a series of gear failures in quick succession that left us limping along with three reefs in the main and a storm jib. While taking a second reef in the mainsail, the downhaul attaching the jib furler to the foredeck broke and began thrashing around out to leeward. The main was in between reefs, neither up nor down, so we had to turn the boat downwind and try and clear up the mess, whilst watching the miles we had fought so hard for slip away from us.

"But there was more. Having managed to reset a jib we were off and running at some sort of reasonable pace until, a few minutes later, it began to rip apart. So we ended up using the storm jib—underpowered and unable to go upwind properly."

The combined forces of the wind, seas, and the yacht smashing its way to windward at a remarkable 11 knots made this the most violent upwind sailing most competitors had ever experienced. The yachts were literally crash landing onto the 3-metre-high waves every minute or so. It was like being aboard a locomotive with square wheels. Adding to the suffering was the ferocity of the rain: "At times it felt like you were getting your face peeled," said Mark Christensen. The wind was so savage that many yachts were using the third reef in the mainsail—making the sail as small as possible—for the first time in the race.

On approach to Ambrose Light, where the fleet would turn left towards the Hudson River and New York City, *ABN AMRO ONE* had done everything expected of her and led by 17 nautical miles. All interest then focussed on the fight for second and third. Only 2 nautical miles separated *The Black Pearl*, *movistar*, *Brasil 1,* and *Ericsson*. *Brasil 1* had come back into the action after being forced to stop soon after sunrise. At first light the crew had looked aft and noticed they were being followed by two long lines and large floats—lines from two crab pots that had been snagged by the keel hours earlier when they were exiting the Chesapeake Bay in darkness. The yacht was brought to a halt so crewman André Fonseca could plunge into the 10-degree water and cut the lines free.

When *ABN AMRO ONE* cruised past the Statue of Liberty in the early morning light and claimed first place at the finish line set immediately adjacent to Lower Manhattan's financial district, the incredibly intense brawl for the minor places continued to brew in her wake. Eventually it was *The Black Pearl* that broke from the pack and sailed home 40 minutes behind the winner. Just astern *Ericsson* was looking set to take third—until *Brasil 1's* veteran navigator, Marcel van Trieste, deftly guided the yacht through a dangerous shoal in the river and gained enough ground to slip into third spot. At the finish only 14 minutes separated second and fifth-placed *movistar*, which was less than 2 minutes behind *Ericsson*.

At the finish only 14 minutes separated the second- and fifth-placed boats.

Left: Ericsson passing under the Verrazano Bridge and finishing fourth in New York.
Above: ABN AMRO ONE skipper Mike Sanderson sprays champagne after adding another leg win to their tally.
Below: The Black Pearl finishes leg six with the Statue of Liberty in the background.

Leg 6 Results

Leg Position	Yacht	Elapsed Time	Leg Points	Baltimore In-Port Race Points	Previous Points	Overall Points	Overall Standing
1	ABN AMRO ONE	1d 15h 7m	7.0	1.0	62.5	70.5	1
2	The Black Pearl	1d 17h 47m	6.0	2.5	39.0	47.5	2
3	Brasil 1	1d 17h 56m	5.0	3.0	34.0	42.0	4
4	Ericsson	1d 17h 59m	4.0	2.0	28.5	34.5	6
5	movistar	1d 18h 1m	3.0	3.5	40.5	47.0	3
6	Brunel*	1d 19h 41m	2.0	0.5	0	2.5	7
7	ABN AMRO TWO	1d 20h 36m	1.0	1.5	39.5	42.0	4

*Brunel re-entered the event after extensive modifications and in so doing her previous points were not counted.

A support boat approaches
ABN AMRO TWO *to take*
the movistar *crew ashore.*

"We have a sailor's code that is an unspoken knowledge of the risks we take going to sea, and that, should we meet our fate, we imagine what we would say if it was us: 'Carry on for me, and help teach others to learn from me how to save other sailors' lives.'"
Mark Rudiger, navigator, *Ericsson*

For Mike "Moose" Sanderson, skipper of *ABN AMRO ONE,* the completion of the 3,200-nautical-mile stage from New York to Portsmouth in England promised the fulfilment of two dreams. On reaching the finish he would claim one of the most emphatic victories in the 33-year history of the event—Black Betty would be unbeatable on points with two legs remaining. At the same time the yacht was his "wedding carriage," transporting him across the Atlantic to where, a few days later, he would wed his fianceé, Scottish solo round-the-world yachtswoman, Emma Richards MBE.

There are times when the North Atlantic can be just as wild and threatening as the hostile Southern Ocean, and there was

Leg07
New York to Portsmouth

Above: Mike Sanderson and the crew of ABN AMRO ONE *wave goodbye to New York's North Cove Marina.*

little doubt that much of leg seven was going to be tough. The welcome mat certainly wouldn't be out: it would be cold, miserable, and gruelling upwind sailing for the first 1,000 nautical miles or more. After that the crews expected to enjoy a fast downwind blast, and while a trans-Atlantic record wasn't in the cards, a world-record 24-hour run of around 580 nautical miles was possible.

The start in New York offered a pleasant diversion for thousands of deskbound office workers in the towering buildings encompassing tiny North Cove Marina, where the yachts had been docked. A large, white, U.S. Coast Guard sailing ship was anchored midstream on the Hudson River to mark the offshore end of the start line, and in the minutes leading up to the 1-minute gun a New York Fire Department fire float sent jets of red, white, and blue water more than 100 feet into the air in a salute to the fleet. All the

Top: The sail turtles with the headsails on the foredecks of the boats ready to leave the dock for the start of leg seven.

Below: ABN AMRO ONE *and* Ericsson *in close battle at the start.*

Above: Hiking hard on board ABN AMRO ONE *after the start of leg seven.*

Right: Ericsson *enters the Solent in gale force conditions.*

time Bouwe Bekking and the crew of *movistar* were watching impatiently from the shore, waiting out a 2-hour penalty that was imposed because they required outside assistance during the pitstop to repair the broken primary winch system.

The trick at the start was not to be trapped by the light offshore wind that was swirling around the tall buildings, but both ABN AMRO boats did just that. *The Black Pearl* was first to scoot away towards the turning mark off the Statue of Liberty. In close pursuit was *Brunel* (which had Englishman Matt Humphries replacing Grant Wharington as skipper), then *Ericsson* and *Brasil 1*. When both ABN AMRO boats finally began to move they were a mile behind, but for Black Betty that wasn't the case for long: "She pinned back her ears and we made our way to the front of the fleet," said Sanderson in his first radio report.

Within 24 hours of leaving New York, the first taste of the promised punishment was being felt. The *Ericsson* crew were wearing every item of clothing they had while Simon Fisher's prediction from *ABN AMRO TWO* that "things are going to get pretty nasty" wasn't wrong.

A short time later, in a wind of 25 knots, the yachts were pushing upwind at 11 knots, launching themselves off waves then smashing into the troughs that followed with a shuddering crash—and no one was prepared to back off the pace. There was also fog in the mix, more like clam chowder than pea soup, said Paul Cayard. This brought the added danger of a collision with

the hundreds of fishing boats working the area. *Brunel* went within a boat length of a crab boat, the fishermen apparently oblivious to her presence.

On day four of what was expected to be a 9-day leg, the cold was really taking its toll. Bouwe Bekking sent out an appeal to race organisers: "Can we please go back to the Southern Ocean? It's freezing, freezing cold here. The Southern Ocean has now lost its reputation among the *movistar* crew for being cold."

Movistar was committed to a course to the north, but *ABN AMRO ONE* soon wasn't. "We decided that we had to bite the bullet and get out of there," said Sanderson, "so we've rocketed from one end of the leader board to the other by having to get out of the north. Now we're last and have a tough fight on our hands." But drama was to follow: "We hit a whale and the boat stopped dead," was the next message from the skipper. "It was dark; there was just no way that we could see it or it could see us, but we do know it was a whale because the tail literally came out of the water and down the side of the boat. It appeared to swim away, so I guess that, after a few headache pills, it will

Left: Brunel, Ericsson, and Brasil 1 *pass beneath the Verrazano Bridge at the start.*
Below: The crew of Ericsson *keep a close eye on* ABN AMRO TWO *in the misty flog as they make their way across the Atlantic.*

The forecast was for 35–40 knots of wind from the west, with gusts likely to reach 50 knots at times, possibly more.

be fine. The impact sheared off one of our daggerboards and has done some damage around the daggerboard case. We've managed to stop and put in the spare daggerboard so now we're back up to 100 percent."

By day six the yachts had sailed out of the Labrador Current and into the Gulf Stream where the water temperature had climbed from 3 degrees to a warm 19.5 degrees Celsius. This, in a way, was disappointing news for the *Brasil 1* team: it meant that the men from tropical Brazil would not get to see their first-ever iceberg.

Both *ABN AMRO ONE* and *Ericsson* were looking fast in the south and Paul Cayard could see that: "*ABN AMRO ONE* has sailed a very smart leg so far. I always said it didn't matter where they went but this time they definitely figured out the weather better than the rest of us. This is the type of weather scenario where the rich get richer, so *ABN AMRO ONE* and

The Medic: The Volvo Ocean Race 2005–06 saw Timo Malinen, from Finland, back for the second time as the race's medical officer. Even with 4 years of planning and preparation, Malinen was going into the unknown with the introduction of the Volvo Open 70.

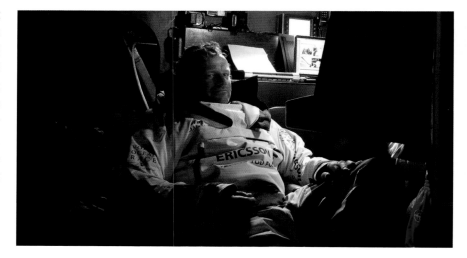

"With these boats being so much faster, we are prepared for different types of injuries," he said on the eve of the race. "There were limits as to how fast a Volvo Ocean 60 would go last time, no matter how hard you pushed it, but the only limit I see this time is the crew—what level of punishment can they absorb before they have to back off? With the Volvo Open 70 being easily capable of 30 knots plus, there's plenty of potential for injury. They can stick their bow into a nasty wave when travelling at that speed and stop almost immediately. It's like having a car crash at more than 20 miles per hour, and people get injured in crashes at that speed.

"We are also prepared for more trauma. Research by an American doctor who knows the subject and was involved with the last race said the stress levels our boys faced through the Southern Ocean were equivalent to being on the front line in a war. At the end of one Southern Ocean leg we had about half of the 97 sailors in tears: tough guys saying they couldn't go through it again. Mind you, some are back again this time. It's amazing how the human mind blocks out certain things."

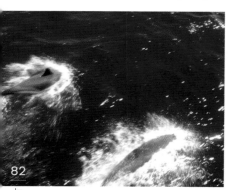

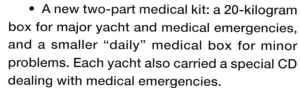

The research by Malinen and his team into previous races was responsible for some compulsory changes and many recommendations for this race, including modifications to features of the yacht design. They included:

• Expanding the training for the two crew members on each yacht who took on the role of onboard medics. They needed to be able to do suturing, create plaster casts, administer IV fluids, and do basic dental work. They had to attend a compulsory training course (some actually trained in hospitals) to meet race requirements.

• An expanded medical manual dealing with everything from back pain (the most common problem) through to sleep deprivation, nutrition, and dehydration.

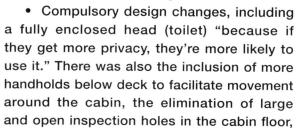

• A new two-part medical kit: a 20-kilogram box for major yacht and medical emergencies, and a smaller "daily" medical box for minor problems. Each yacht also carried a special CD dealing with medical emergencies.

• Compulsory design changes, including a fully enclosed head (toilet) "because if they get more privacy, they're more likely to use it." There was also the inclusion of more handholds below deck to facilitate movement around the cabin, the elimination of large and open inspection holes in the cabin floor, the installation of longer bunks, and a minimum ceiling height in the navigation station. Crew also wear lightweight fibreglass helmets for head protection when exposed to dangerous situations, like going up the mast in rough weather. A minimum diameter for the steering wheels was also recommended to reduce the possibility of cramp.

Explaining his role in preparing for the race, Malinen said: "We're not the police with much of what we do. We're not trying to be Big Brother. We're just advising them as experts, showing that there are other ways of thinking about what they will face."

Ericsson should be in good shape." In realising that the leg was now going to take longer than anticipated, the Pirates of the Caribbean team started rationing food.

Brunel watch captain Jeff Scott, a veteran of 14 Atlantic crossings, commented on day seven that the weather pattern for this time of the year was the most unusual he had seen, and the next forecast showed no respite: an uncharacteristic low-pressure system would give the yachts a wild ride over the next 2 days. The forecast was for 35–40 knots of wind from the west, with gusts likely to reach 50 knots at times, possibly more.

Around 0200 on day eight, May 18, the *ABN AMRO TWO* crew felt the first hint of the new weather front. The yacht was 1,300 nautical miles from the finish and in fifth place when the wind strengthened quickly from 12 to 25 knots, leading skipper Sebastien Josse to call for an immediate sail change. With that task completed the team got back into full racing mode. Josse was steering, Hans Horrevoets was sitting on the stack of sails on the starboard side trimming the spinnaker, and Nick Bice, Simeon Tienpont, Andrew Lewis, and Lucas Brun were manning the winches. Those on deck

From left: The Black Pearl *powers towards England.*

Big seas and high winds for Brasil 1.

were in the process of rotating positions so each could go below in turn and put on his safety harness. Hans was the only one left to complete the mission when, in an instant, *ABN AMRO TWO* ploughed into the wave ahead at around 25 knots, nose-diving as it rolled to windward. A powerful wall of water roared aft, slamming into all on deck and engulfing them: it was as if the yacht was a submarine doing a crash dive. When the bow burst through the other side of the wave and the yacht resurfaced, the spinnaker was uncontrolled and flapping. Instinctively the crew wound the winches but nothing happened. "Where is Hans? Where is Hans?" Josse screamed with great alarm. "Man overboard! Man overboard!"

Scott Beavis ran to the man overboard equipment (the Jon Buoy) at the stern and released it while Tienpont grabbed the life ring and threw that overboard. Others rushed to get the spinnaker down. Below deck, navigator Simon Fisher hammered the "man overboard" button on the GPS unit in the navigation station to mark the search area. He then typed a hurried message, which burst onto the computer screen at race headquarters: "Man overboard, man overboard," were the dreaded words he tapped out, and then he detailed the situation. Instantly the operations room at the Volvo Ocean Race headquarters near Portsmouth activated its well-rehearsed emergency procedure. The yachts closest to *ABN AMRO TWO*—*movistar*, *The Black Pearl*, *Brasil 1*, and *Brunel*—were directed to change course to the search area. At the same time, race officials were woken from their sleep and summoned to HQ.

Simon Fisher: "We were only 1.6 nautical miles away from Hans when we had the spinnaker down, the boat turned around, and were on a course back to him. It was really, really impressive. The guys on deck had searchlights ready. Simeon Tienpont had put on his diving gear so he could get into the water if needed. We motored back upwind as it was too hard to sail in 37 knots of breeze. After about half a mile we found the first life ring we had thrown over the side—we had put as much stuff in the water as we could to make it as easy as possible to find Hans. Half a mile away we found another life ring and, at two-tenths of a mile, we found

Noel Drennan and Mike Joubert show their frustration while repairing their mainsail on board movistar.

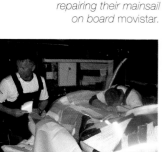

Clockwise from top: Full foul weather clothing and helmets are required on board Brunel *as they sail in extreme weather.*

On board Ericsson *the speeds are starting to climb and spray is flying as the wind and waves pick up.*

ABN AMRO ONE 162 miles to the finish.

A powerful wall of water roared aft, slamming into all on deck and engulfing them: it was as if the yacht was a submarine doing a crash dive. When the yacht resurfaced, the spinnaker was uncontrolled and flapping.

"Where is Hans? Where is Hans?" Josse screamed with great alarm. "Man overboard! Man overboard!"

the 'Jon Buoy.' Shortly thereafter we spotted a personal strobe light and found Hans."

Horrevoets had been in the water around 40 minutes when he was recovered. There was no sign of a pulse.

"By the time we found Hans, we saw he was drowned," Tienpont said. "George Peet went for all the CPR (cardio pulmonary resuscitation) equipment. We had Hans downstairs within a minute of getting him on deck and five of us tried to resuscitate him, checking on each other, keeping the right pace, being as professional as we could. We tried to warm him up."

Race organisers on shore linked the *ABN AMRO TWO* crew with the Accident and Emergency Department at Derriford Hospital in Plymouth, United Kingdom, by radio so all relevant information could be relayed from doctors. After 90 minutes CPR was stopped.

The shocking, tragic news of Hans' death was radioed to all competing yachts. "We couldn't believe it," said *ABN AMRO ONE's* Justin Slattery. "We all just sat around the navigation station in stunned silence. We didn't know what to say or do."

With Hans' body placed inside a watertight compartment, the emotionally shattered *ABN AMRO TWO* crew then tried to regain some composure and turn the yacht towards England. "It was a few hours before we got going again," said Simon Fisher. "We stopped and tidied up our boat, then it took an hour to take stock, sit down together as a crew and talk a little. An hour later we were sailing again—at a steady pace, not race pace. As the hours went by we became eager to get back into our normal watch system, and a day later we were back to sailing at full speed."

With all yachts back into racing mode *ABN AMRO ONE* then held a 174-nautical-mile lead over *Ericsson*. It was a large enough gap for Sanderson to have his team sail conservatively, but the weather on the final night threw out one last test: "It's been a night of heinous action," the skipper reported. "The hours of darkness have been super stressful trying to keep the boat under 28 knots and not hurtle out of the next wave. The maximum wind speed was 51 knots and the seas are getting massive as we get closer to the English Channel. I'm counting down the miles. It's time to finish this one."

"We couldn't believe it. We all just sat around the navigation station in stunned silence. We didn't know what to say or do." Justin Slattery, crewmember, *ABN AMRO ONE*

Above: Hans Horrevoets and Simeon Tienpont pose as ABN AMRO TWO passes Cape Horn.

Left and right: Hans Horrevoets.

Hans Horrevoets 1974–2006

The infectious laugh is no more, and there will be a void in the lives of all who knew Hans Horrevoets.

Nothing could dull his enthusiasm for either sailing or his family, as was so clearly demonstrated when *ABN AMRO TWO* sailed into Baltimore at the end of the leg from Rio de Janeiro. His first priority, the moment the yacht arrived, was to leap onto the dock and hug his pregnant partner and their child, and to share some special moments with them. With that complete he turned to the media scrum: it was suggested that he must be devastated after the yacht had finished in last place on the leg: "Why devastated? We are very competitive and love to do well, but I have been away and now I'm going to see my beautiful family. In a few days I'll go sailing again. Nice life!" The trademark laugh followed and there were no more questions.

He was the eternal optimist in this race: he could only see the bright side, the right side. And there were just two ingredients in his essence of life: his family—partner Petra and their baby daughter Bobbi—and sailing.

Hans, aged 32 and the oldest member of the *ABN AMRO TWO* crew, was once again living out a childhood dream when he perished: "As a child, I just had one goal in my life: sailing regattas!" he wrote on his web site. "My biggest dream was sailing The Whitbread Round The World Race. Racing around the world on a Whitbread 60 was my largest passion. Attending crew selections, traineeships at Quantum Sails and North Sails, and many visits to a fitness centre helped me make my dream come true in 1997–98. As a trimmer and a sailmaker on board *BrunelSunergy* I sailed all legs. I was only 22 years old when the race began. This was an experience no one can ever take away from me!"

His original role with the *ABN AMRO TWO* team was as a member of the crew selection panel. It was a position that allowed him to help others achieve their own dream of harnessing the wind and circumnavigating the globe under sail. Then, at the last minute, a crew position became vacant, and Hans needed no time to consider the invitation to go again.

The man knew the dangers he would be facing, and he accepted them: "It can be scary, yes," he told journalist Riath Al-Samarrai before the start in Sanxenxo. "But it is why we race. The families get more worried than we do. This is just what we do. The guys are all excellent sailors and this, for them, is a big chance to make a name for themselves. Yes, it can be dangerous, of course it can, but what if we didn't sail? Life would be boring."

Above: A portrait of Hans Horrevoets on the bow of ABN AMRO TWO *in Cape Town.*

Left: Hans Horrevoets, his partner Petra, and their daughter Bobbi together in Melbourne before the start of leg three.

The grief-stricken *ABN AMRO TWO* team had, without hesitation, turned back and were standing by *movistar*, following in its wake only boat lengths away.

More than 500 nautical miles behind the leader the crew of *movistar* was anxiously watching another nasty low-pressure system that was moving towards them. They were expecting it to be extremely tough going, but they got the unexpected.

"We were sailing in 25–28 knots of breeze and big, 5–6 metre seas," said Bouwe Bekking, "when all of sudden we heard a loud 'crack,' so we immediately turned the boat downwind. We soon found that water was streaming in around the keel hinge and that the keel pin had moved 50 millimetres sideways in the structure."

The problem was extremely serious—possibly terminal. The motion of the yacht in the big seas meant that the keel might rip away from the yacht, causing the boat to capsize and flip upside down. Navigator Andrew Cape activated the Inmarsat C terminal and sent a crisis message to alert race headquarters of *movistar's* predicament and request that emergency services be put on standby. *Brunel* and *ABN AMRO TWO*, the closest yachts, were asked to change course towards *movistar's* position.

"It was pretty hard to ask the *ABN AMRO TWO* boys to come back as they already had plenty on their plate," Bekking reported from their stricken yacht. "*Brunel* had their own issues so we have agreed to delay our decision on needing their assistance. We are just keeping our fingers crossed the boat will hold out and that we can bring it safely into port."

ABN AMRO TWO *is accompanied by the Dutch navy towards Falmouth, southwest England.*

Right: The movistar crew are transferred into a RIB and taken to Falmouth.

Left: A dejected
Bouwe Bekking.
Right: ABN AMRO
ONE passing the
scoring gate at Lizard
Point, England.

Hours later, after Bekking and Cape further analysed the intensity of the approaching storm, it was realised that it would be too dangerous to remain aboard *movistar*. They were 300 nautical miles from England, the safety of the crew was paramount, and it was almost a certainty that the yacht could not survive the brutal seas and 50-knot winds that were bearing down on them. The trouble-plagued yacht would have to be abandoned.

"The hardest decision I have ever taken in my life was the call to abandon ship." Bouwe Bekking, skipper, *movistar*

The grief-stricken *ABN AMRO TWO* team had, without hesitation, turned back and were standing by *movistar*, following in its wake only boat lengths away. Once the decision had been made to "abandon ship," Seb Josse took control and executed a pluperfect rescue. The *movistar* crew, along with a spare life raft and their personal equipment, were transferred to Josse's yacht using another life raft. When the two crews were aboard and united as one, there was high emotion all round. Soon the 19 sailors turned their backs on the sinking *movistar* and sailed away, all the time knowing that the real sorrow was with Hans Horrevoets' pregnant partner, Petra, and 1-year-old daughter back in The Netherlands.

Meanwhile the British Royal Navy had also responded to the *movistar* emergency, sending *HMS Mersey* to rendezvous with *ABN AMRO TWO* and shepherd it through the storm. It brought some comfort for all aboard.

"The hardest decision I have ever taken in my life was the call to abandon ship," Bekking radioed from aboard *ABN AMRO TWO*. "In the end I took the tough decision—10 lives at

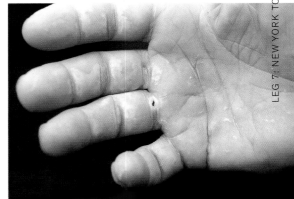

Left: ABN AMRO ONE skipper
Mike Sanderson, elated after
winning leg seven.

Above: The wear and tear on
David Rolfe's right hand after 2
weeks at sea on board Ericsson.

Clockwise from below:
ABN AMRO ONE arrives in
Gunwharf Quays after
crossing the finish line.

A shattered, but relieved,
Mike Sanderson at the end
of the leg in Portsmouth.

The Black Pearl ploughs
towards the
finish in a gale.

stake along with a similar number of families. It was the right call. There is no mirror on board here, but if I could face myself, I would know that we have done everything possible.

"Seb and his crew have been fantastic. We all realised that turning around had been a very hard call for them, and hopefully they can find a little comfort in that they have saved 10 lives. A boat is just a boat. You can replace it, but lives you cannot."

Four days after the loss of Hans Horrevoets, *ABN AMRO TWO* was met by the Royal Netherlands naval frigate, *HNLMS Van Galen*, off Falmouth and his body was transferred for repatriation to his homeland. Sebastien Josse and his crew bid an emotional farewell to their teammate, holding a minute's silence on deck before the transfer took place. A short time earlier the *movistar* crew had been collected by a support boat and transported to shore.

For the crew of race leader *ABN AMRO ONE,* their late-night victory off Portsmouth should have been a moment of great euphoria. They had arguably scored the most emphatic outright victory in the 33-year history of the race. Wearing black armbands, they arrived at the dock at Gunwharf

On shore the teams from other race yachts, along with family and friends, lined a nearby dock, holding hands or with arms around shoulders in a show of silent solidarity as *ABN AMRO TWO* approached.

Quays to a welcome delicately balanced between grief and celebration.

While obviously burdened by the loss of an ABN AMRO team member, Sanderson had to reflect on his remarkable achievement: "It is amazing really. It is such a special moment. For me this is my Olympic medal, my climbing of Everest. It's a childhood dream to have skippered a boat and won the Volvo Ocean Race. I have been trying to hold back my emotions this whole race and now I can let them out."

Ericsson turned in their best offshore effort of the race by finishing second ahead of *The Black Pearl,* with *Brasil 1* and *Brunel* next. But it was the arrival of *ABN AMRO TWO* that was needed, and when it came the hundreds of people gathered on the waterfront were anxious to bring some

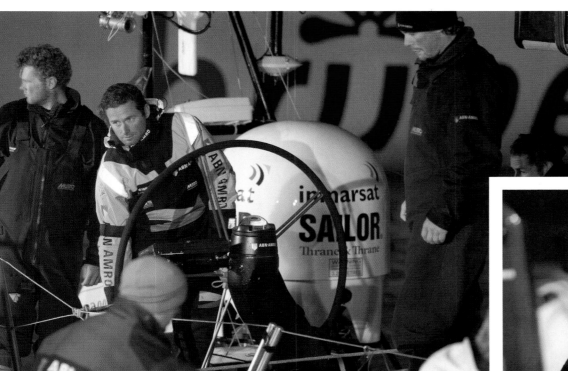

Clockwise from below left, opposite page: Crowds line the dock in Portsmouth awaiting the arrival of *ABN AMRO TWO*.

A tired and emotional crew of *ABN AMRO TWO* bring the white boat alongside the dock in Portsmouth.

Mike Sanderson hugs Sebastien Josse as soon as the French skipper steps ashore.

Sebastien Josse at the *ABN AMRO TWO* press conference held in Portsmouth.

Simeon Tienpont receives a hug when *ABN AMRO TWO* arrives in Portsmouth.

warmth to an otherwise bleak English evening. They wanted to show their support and share the crews' emotion, but no one was quite sure how.

On approach to the dock there was a spiritual, almost eerie moment for the *ABN AMRO TWO* crew. They told of a white swan that emerged out of the night sky, glided towards them and landed off the bow. It then swam ahead as if guiding them to safety.

On shore the teams from other race yachts, along with family and friends, lined a nearby dock, holding hands or with arms around shoulders in a show of silent solidarity as *ABN AMRO TWO* approached. When the white, black, and gold hull appeared out of the blackness and into the glare of the dock-side floodlights there were nine lonely men on deck and their eyes reflected the tears that they carried. Immediately it seemed everyone was shedding tears. The empathy was overwhelming. Then someone started clapping, and it was infectious. Within seconds the applause spread like a wave across the entire crowd on the promenade and along the docks, and suddenly there was an element of relief in the air. "The Kids" were home. But they were no longer kids: they were men, and they were heroes.

Leg 7 Results

Leg Position	Yacht	Elapsed Time	Leg Points	Scoring Gate Points	Redress Points*	Previous Points	Overall Points	Overall Standing
1	ABN AMRO ONE	9d 6h 30m	7.0	3.5		70.5	81.0	1
2	Ericsson	9d 19h 26m	6.0	3.0		34.5	43.5	6
3	The Black Pearl	9d 19h 54m	5.0	2.5	1.5	47.5	56.5	2
4	Brasil 1	9d 21h 30m	4.0	2.0	1.5	42.0	49.5	3
5	Brunel	10d 17h 16m	3.0	1.5		2.5	7.0	7
6	ABN AMRO TWO	11d 2h 8m	2.0	1.0	1.5	42.0	46.5	5
7	movistar	did not finish	1.0	0.0		47.0	48.0	4

*for turning back to assist other boats

"Hans Horrevoets' passing and *movistar's* problems got into our heads in Portsmouth. No one can say that they didn't analyse the situation and say, 'that could be me.' We all wondered if it was worth it. We know that sailing has some degree of risk, and that sailing the Volvo Ocean Race makes it even riskier, but I wouldn't blame anyone for having second thoughts about sailing this leg, especially with the possibility of facing similar conditions to leg seven. But I think it is worth it. We all love sailing." André Fonseca, crewmember, *Brasil 1*

There was a little-known piece of race history linked to the departure of the fleet from the dock at Gunwharf Quays in Portsmouth for the start of leg eight to Rotterdam. The classic old waterfront pub that the yachts were passing at the harbour entrance, the Still & West, was where, in 1971, Colonel Bill Whitbread and Admiral Otto Steiner enjoyed a few beers and brewed the idea that became the Whitbread Round The World Race, what is now the Volvo Ocean Race.

There were also shades of The Whitbread race starts from that era once the yachts were out on the Solent. Hundreds of spectator craft had gathered to farewell them while an

Leg08
Portsmouth
to Rotterdam

Far left: Close quarter contact during the in-port race in Portsmouth.

Left: ABN AMRO TWO passing the Needles after the start.

Clockwise from top:
Clouds form over
Ericsson.
ABN AMRO ONE
during the in-port race
in Portsmouth.
The bow of Brunel
slices throught
the water.

equally enthusiastic crowd lined the nearby shore where the backdrop was Southsea Castle, a bold, grey stone bastion built by Henry VIII in 1544 to protect that part of the coastline from invaders.

The 1,500-nautical-mile stretch to Rotterdam would take the yachts to the west through the Solent, out into the Celtic Sea, up the coast of Ireland and then across to the top of Scotland before turning towards the finish. This region holds a reputation for mustering abominable weather on a regular basis, a fact that had many sailors predicting that leg eight could be the toughest of the nine stages. Instead though, in the hours leading up to the start, the crews had been preparing for a marathon. It appeared that after dishing out a battering of monumental proportions on the previous trans-Atlantic leg, the powers of nature had decided to make amends and take a rest. The weather analysis showed that this would be the slowest leg so far: a "drifter" where it would take at least 6 days to cover a distance that these yachts could easily achieve in half the time, given strong winds.

The skipper most frustrated by the forecast was *movistar's* Bouwe Bekking—and he wasn't on the water. The search for his yacht, which had been abandoned 400 nautical miles out in the Atlantic 2 weeks earlier, had been called off. It had apparently sunk. Up until then *movistar* had been

Within 20 minutes of the start, all the action had come to a standstill: the breeze had evaporated, and unbeknown to the crews, they had just experienced the strongest wind they'd see for the next 1,500 miles.

locked into a fight for a podium finish in the overall results, and she was a proven light-weather flyer.

As the start gun boomed out its signal, the six yachts swept into the line like a squadron of well-coordinated aerobatic aircraft. Simultaneously the on-water spectators saw this signal as an invitation to join the action: every high-speed boat wanted to be ringside as part of the escort flotilla.

But within 20 minutes of the start all the action had come to a standstill. The breeze had evaporated, and unbeknown to the crews, they had just experienced the strongest wind they'd see for the next 1,500 miles.

Torben Grael's *Brasil 1* was the bright star leaving the Solent, but the local knowledge and newfound form aboard *Ericsson* saw her take the lead after rock hopping along the shore on the first night. It was slow going, so slow that some yachts actually anchored to counter an adverse tide. As a consequence, only 120 nautical miles were covered in the first 20 hours, normally a 6-hour run in ideal conditions.

Each yacht had its moment of glory on the stretch to Land's End and into the Celtic Sea. As they passed the Scilly Isles the spread from first to last was only 8 nautical

miles, with *Ericsson* and *The Black Pearl* level pegging at the front. The next target was the legendary Fastnet Rock, 120 nautical miles away off the coast of Ireland, and it was on this stretch that the first strategic play of this game was made. The three Farr designs—*Ericsson, The Black Pearl,* and *Brasil 1*—decided on the direct route: they would try to punch their way through the light winds associated with the high-pressure system that was blocking the way. At the same time the tacticians on the three others, *Brunel* and the two ABN AMRO boats, decided to go to the northeast in a bid to sail around the problem. It meant covering a greater distance, but there was a big chance they would see more wind and sail faster.

ABN AMRO ONE's navigator, Stan Honey, became increasingly convinced that this was the right move as this trio gathered momentum. It had the hallmarks of being a brilliant strategy, until yet again it was proved that weather forecasting is not an exact science.

The high pressure moved unexpectedly and everything changed: "There was a modest reward for us instead of a big gain," Honey declared. "At least we got back into the pack. But if the high had stayed where it was then there was a chance we would have been 'launched'—the other

Above: Five of the six boats take the seaward side of the course at the start of leg eight.

Left: Back down the Solent, past Hurst Spit lighthouse and out to sea.

The Pigeon: This is the story of *ABN AMRO TWO* and a pigeon, a bird that in some parts of Europe is considered an omen for good fortune. It comes as a consequence of the tragic loss of *ABN AMRO TWO* crewman Hans Horrevoets on the wild, 3,200-nautical-mile leg from New York to Portsmouth.

It encompasses the decision by skipper Sebastien Josse and his young team to continue racing in the Volvo Ocean Race. This decision was partly influenced by Hans' father, who suggested that his son would want it no other way. They would race in Hans' memory.

As they departed the dock and headed for the starting area at the eastern end of the Solent it was obvious that the crew was glad to be back in the saddle.

Their determination to acquit themselves well was evident from the moment the countdown to the start began. There was no holding back. The yacht was dancing to every command that came from Josse as he spun the

Below: ABN AMRO TWO *during the in-port race, Portsmouth.*
Right: The pigeon sailing on board ABN AMRO TWO.

wheel, all the time looking for a gap between boats on the start line. The very popular Frenchman, whose stature reminds one of Napoleon Bonaparte, was bounding from side to side in the cockpit, leaping from one steering wheel to the other with the agility of a gymnast on a trampoline. The crew responded with perfect sail trim, and, when the desired gap between the starting boat and stablemate *ABN AMRO ONE* opened up, Josse had his charge driving for it as though it was a giant wedge. It was a perfectly executed start.

There was a good sailing breeze of 15–18 knots, and a promise of more to come. The Needles, some 14 miles away upwind, was reporting 30 knots, and the low, rain-bearing black clouds to the west confirmed that it was coming their way.

Just as they were settling down for the 2-mile upwind leg, and, within a minute of the start gun sounding, a pigeon descended from the heavens and landed in the helmsman's cockpit, immediately behind Seb. Initial thoughts that it might be exhausted and undernourished were quickly debunked. This bird was very much at home and appeared to know exactly what it was doing.

After checking out those nearby, the bird nonchalantly moved to the windward side of the cockpit and settled comfortably under the helmsman's platform that Seb was standing on. When it came time to tack, one would have expected that the commotion and violent motion associated with the manoeuvre would unsettle the feathered guest and it would fly off. But no: it calmly emerged from under the steering platform and, like all good sailors, moved to the high side, again taking up residence under Seb's platform. It was as if it knew that weight to windward contributed to boat speed.

Not surprisingly, the word "Hans" was heard in whispered tones in the cockpit.

Not surprisingly, the word "Hans" was heard in whispered tones in the cockpit.

Incredibly, the bird would make its move from side to side each time the yacht tacked or gybed. And each time a bad wave threw the yacht around, the bird would retract its landing gear as if it was second nature, squatting low on the deck so it could retain a better grip.

The eager anticipation held for an exhilarating downwind ride during this race was quickly met. A perfect spinnaker set at the first mark was followed by remarkable acceleration in the building breeze . . . the numbers on the speedo rolled over like the symbols on a slot machine—15 knots, 16, 18, 20, 22, 23.8. Incredible—yet this was only a morsel of what this crew had experienced offshore. Imagine what it must have been like when they set the world monohull 24-hour record of 563 nautical miles, charging down the face of giant waves at better than 30 knots!

The race continued as a procession until just after the boat rounded the windward mark for the second time. Another squall came through and *Ericsson's* spinnaker snagged on the side rail, causing it to explode into pieces. The sail ripped from bottom to top before remnants fluttered into the water. It would prove to be an expensive problem in more ways than one. *ABN AMRO TWO* quickly grabbed the opportunity and surfed past *Ericsson* to take up fourth place. Then, almost ironically, the same opportunity opened up in front for *ABN AMRO ONE*. *The Black Pearl* broached in a squall and in an instant its spinnaker was shredded. That was the break *ABN AMRO ONE* needed and she quickly took the lead.

There were no more place changes through to the finish on a day where the crews were tested in everything between 7 and 34 knots of wind. It was a day of great sailing.

When the finish came the *ABN AMRO TWO* men had done themselves proud. They were back on track and had much to look forward to. Fourth place was a highly creditable result. There were smiles all round.

As the sails were lowered and the yacht turned towards Plymouth the pigeon emerged from under Seb's steering platform, strutted with confidence to the stern, had one last look around, then flew off towards land.

Left: Bowmen on ABN AMRO TWO *working hard during the in-port race.*

Above: Brunel's memorial wreath for Hans Horrevoets on deck.

Ericsson *passing Hurst Castle at the western entrance to the Solent in the early stages of leg eight.*

three yachts would have parked for a day and we could well have won the leg by 200 miles."

The drift continued towards Fastnet Rock, something that presented the crews with new opportunities to entertain themselves. This was life at the other extreme:

Simon Fisher, *ABN AMRO TWO:* "I couldn't really imagine it getting much lighter. The sea is like glass, the sky clear blue, and the boat is quietly ghosting through the water. We have had a bit of a race on today, against a flock of seagulls that easily swam up to us and had a look at what was going on. I think it would have been easier for us to ride their bow wave as opposed to them riding ours!"

Andrew Cape, now the latest navigator on boad *Ericsson:* "The fleet is definitely heading for a record run in the next 24 hours for the shortest distance travelled."

Horacio Carabelli, *Brasil 1:* "It is hard to believe that 3 weeks ago we were sailing these waters in 30–40 knot winds and 5-metre waves. Today we had a visit of a pigeon. It walked through the whole boat, even inside. Every time it flew way, some minutes later it was back with us. Let's hope that the voyage is not too long and there is a food shortage because there are sailors already talking about how fat it looks."

It took 4 days for the yachts to reach Fastnet Rock, where only 7 nautical miles separated first from last. The order, if there really was one, was *Brasil 1, Ericsson, Brunel, ABN AMRO TWO, The Black Pearl,* and *ABN AMRO ONE.* For *Brunel's* skipper, Matt Humphries, getting to "the rock" at a snail's pace brought some comparisons: "We've worked out that we have 25 Fastnet Races between us. I was sailing with Ross Field in the Maxi One Design Class when we set the current record for the course. This time sailing to the Fastnet

was the slowest trip up for all of us, even slower than the time I sailed my father's Half Tonner *Min-o-Din* [a yacht less than half the size of a Volvo Open 70] to victory in the 1991 Fastnet."

The plus side to all this was that the gloriously sunny days made for great sightseeing along the picturesque west coast of Ireland and across the top of Scotland. "There are beautiful cliffs off the southwest coast of Ireland," wrote *Ericsson's* Ken Read. "I have to admit that, while staring at the land, I was drooling over the famous Irish golf courses that could be played in this weather." Irish crewmember Damian Foxall helped pass the time for his team-

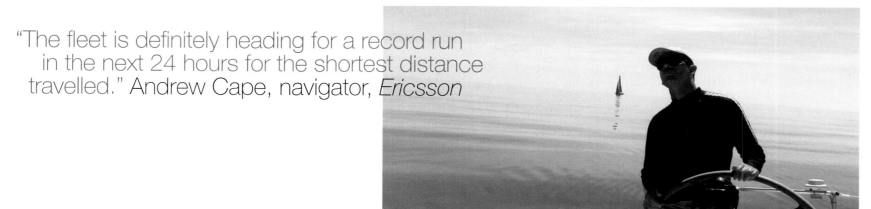

"The fleet is definitely heading for a record run in the next 24 hours for the shortest distance travelled." Andrew Cape, navigator, *Ericsson*

From left: Torben Grael steers Brasil 1 *carefully in millpond conditions with the competition in sight.*

Brasil 1 *leads the fleet away from the Dorset coast.*

Ericsson *manages to maintain some forward motion in the calm and windless conditions in the Irish Sea.*

Brasil 1 scores their first win in Rotterdam.

Below: The Ericsson *crew trim for speed in the race for the finish line.*

mates with a guided tour of the coast: "Dat's where I used to live up 'dere lads! And dere's a cray pot over 'dere. And 'dere's a luvley pub . . ."

The boys from *Brasil 1* found their most memorable experience at night: "What is amazing for us, from the tropics, is how the nights start to get short," reported Horacio Carabelli. "We can see the light from the sun on the horizon during the whole night."

With the crawl continuing, race organisers notified the crews of a change of course at the northern tip of Scotland: The rounding mark of Fair Isle would be changed to Duncansby Head, a savings of 76 nautical miles.

Unfortunately, the northern coast of Scotland turned on cold air, grey skies, and fog. The passage between islands and rocky outcrops in this rugged and remote part of the world, known as Pentland Firth, provided a complicated

Out in front *Ericsson*, *Brasil 1*, and *ABN AMRO ONE* were all in a line, until the "Black Betty" boys found a favourable swirl in the current and were literally washed through to the lead.

equation: it is very narrow and the region has some of the world's fastest flowing tidal currents, up to 16 knots, leaving no room for error. Once you committed to going through the gap there was no turning back. You had to go in harm's way and hope that fate went in your favour.

With the bleak conditions leaving little to see, imaginations ran wild as a result of the names of points of land and tidal swirls encountered: the Butt of Lewis, Cape Wrath, the Swilkie, the Bore of Huna, the Wells of Tuftalie, the Duncansby Bore, the Merry Men of Mey, Muckle Skerry Island. It all led Stan Honey to comment: "If someone wrote a novel and used all of those names, people would say it was incredible. Not even Tolkien could come up with some of those names."

It was at the top of Scotland that the fleet literally split in two. Through no fault of their own the three trailing boats were suddenly on the wrong side of an unexpected and unusual change in the weather. A small

From left: A jubilant Brazilian team celebrate their win.

Portrait of a happy man: Torben Grael, skipper of Brasil 1 after winning leg eight.

ABN AMRO ONE skipper Mike Sanderson sprays champagne as they have won the race overall.

trough developed in the high-pressure system and literally drove a wedge through the middle of the fleet. *The Black Pearl, Brunel,* and *ABN AMRO TWO* were suddenly in a windless hole on the wrong side of this invisible hurdle and missed the ride. In a matter of hours a small deficit in miles between them and the leading trio became an enormous chasm—more than 60 miles.

Brunel's problems didn't end there. As they exited the tricky waters and sailed into the North Sea, they faced a man-made hurdle that they couldn't argue with: "This morning we were making great gains on *The Black Pearl* when we got a call on the VHF radio: 'Sailing Yacht, this is guard ship *St. John*,'" explained navigator Will Oxley. "A huge cable-laying vessel with eight cables streaming 2.5 miles astern of it was ahead of us. We had to make a substantial alteration of course to starboard to avoid the cables. We shaved it as close as possible to round the eight 'trailing buoys' marking the safe passage with about 10 metres to spare, but lost everything we had gained on *The Black Pearl* and *ABN AMRO TWO*. Bugger!"

Apart from a bitterly cold air temperature, it was the dense fog that made the passage across the North Sea less pleasant and quite dangerous: "The situation was so difficult that we almost hit a tug that was on a collision course with us." said *Brasil 1's* Horacio Carabelli. "We couldn't see it on our radar, but we knew it was there because we heard them on the VHF radio. The tug informed us that it was speeding up to pass us to starboard, but the

only thing we saw that proved it was there was the huge wave it created and the smoke from the engines."

For *Brasil 1, ABN AMRO ONE,* and *Ericsson,* it was a drag race to the finish. Having claimed *Ericsson* in what were tailor-made reaching conditions, *ABN AMRO ONE* was carving big chunks out of *Brasil 1's* lead. But "Black Betty" ran out of runway. In the early morning hours of day seven, the boys from Brazil came home to a tumultuous welcome as the winners. The margin of just 3 minutes over "Black Betty" didn't matter: they'd claimed their first big scalp of the race and the party to end all parties was about to begin.

Leg 8 Results

Leg Position	Yacht	Elapsed Time	Leg Points	Portsmouth In-Port Race Points	Previous Points	Overall Points	Overall Standing
1	Brasil 1	7d 6h 48m	7.0	2.5	49.5	59.0	3
2	ABN AMRO ONE	7d 6h 51m	6.0	3.5	81.0	90.5	1
3	Ericsson	7d 7h 17m	5.0	1.5	43.5	50.0	5
4	The Black Pearl	7d 18h 34m	4.0	3.0	56.5	63.5	2
5	ABN AMRO TWO	7d 19h 10m	3.0	2.0	46.5	51.5	4
6	Brunel	7d 20h 17m	2.0	1.0	7.0	10.0	7
7	movistar	did not race	0	0.0	48.0	48.0	6

"Tradition has it that the boat that wins the first leg wins the race. I think that it is quite likely the case, as this is the boat that has done the most preparation. Some of the key decisions that we made in the first year of this campaign, and during the buildup to the start, showed all the way through. A lot of people wrote us off before the start, but we had a lot of confidence in what we had done, and that makes winning a really good feeling."

Mark "Crusty" Christensen, watch captain, *ABN AMRO ONE*

While it might have been an anti-climax, the final leg of the Volvo Ocean Race was in fact a grande finale, a spectacular and fitting tribute to the successful completion of the most demanding of sporting challenges, one where the best offshore sailors had met and matched the ultimate test, the crossing of the world's great oceans in all their fury and finest moods.

It didn't matter that the outright winner was already known, that the stage was a simple 500-nautical-mile coastal sprint from Rotterdam to Göteborg, or that the only true contest in leg nine was for the minor places.

Leg09
Rotterdam
to Göteborg

Far left: Overall winner ABN AMRO ONE powers away from the start of leg nine as crowds of spectator boats struggle to keep pace.

Left: Brunel rounds the windward mark to the rear of the fleet during the Rotterdam in-port race.

Left: Brunel *to the rear of the fleet with* ABN AMRO TWO *during the Rotterdam in-port race.*

Right: Brasil 1 *bears away past the windward mark ahead of rival* The Black Pearl *during a closely fought Rotterdam race.*

The impetus for the leg started with the outstanding success of the Rotterdam stopover. Massive crowds had converged on the quaint little boat harbour at Veerhaven with the sole purpose of viewing the fleet and sharing in the race atmosphere. Rotterdam, the world's busiest commercial port, is located on the Maas, a mighty river that meanders 600 miles from its upper reaches in France to where it meets the ocean just downstream from the city. The Maas links 5 million people and is a scene of high activity around the clock as large, motorised barges literally laden to the gunwales with cargo use it as a maritime highway.

For the support teams and the sailors, the stopover meant special times, especially for those backing the ABN AMRO yachts. This was their home port, and with Mike Sanderson's *ABN AMRO ONE* already declared the outright race winner, and with the young team on *ABN AMRO TWO* having acquitted themselves in such spectacular fashion—including claiming the world

24-hour monohull sailing distance record—there was cause for considerable euphoria. The ABN AMRO enthusiasts had even more to cheer about when the team on *ABN AMRO ONE* demonstrated demoralising light-weather sailing skills and took out the in-port race there by more than 3 minutes from *Brasil 1* and *The Black Pearl*.

The general enthusiasm for the Volvo Ocean Race continued when it came time to depart Rotterdam. Thousands upon thousands of people crammed every vantage point around the small, stonewalled basin to participate in the farewell. Then, as the fleet began the 20-mile parade under sail to the river entrance, a huge flotilla comprising everything from kayaks to sailing ships created an escort. At the same time tens of thousands of locals lined the riverbanks to bid farewell, prompting Paul Cayard to say: "We wore our arms out waving for 2 hours straight."

Off the river entrance a lumpy sea, whipped up by a brisk, chill-laden northerly wind, made conditions far from pleasant. Regardless, more than a dozen square riggers and hundreds of other spectator craft, large and small, ventured offshore to see the yachts set out for the final time on this edition of the race around the world.

From the instant the start gun sounded, it was obvious that there were two theories on the right way to go on the upwind leg to the north. *The Black*

Pearl along with *Ericsson* and *Brunel* speared through the spectator fleet on a very definite mission to get away from the coast on starboard tack. The others, led by Torben Grael's *Brasil 1*, sailed north, parallel to the shore on the opposite tack—except for *ABN AMRO ONE*, which headed back to the start having been recalled for crossing the line before the gun.

The race within this leg was to decide the overall minor places for the route around the planet. *The Black Pearl* had a slender hold on second but could be beaten on total points by *Brasil 1*, depending on where they finished. So there was little surprise, after Torben Grael persisted with his course along the shore (because the wind had shifted in *Brasil 1's* favour earlier than expected), that Cayard decided there was no option but to bail out from

"We wore our arms out waving for 2 hours straight." Paul Cayard, skipper, *The Black Pearl*

Clockwise from left: The Volvo Open 70s in the start of leg nine from Rotterdam to Göteborg.

ABN AMRO ONE *waves goodbye to Rotterdam.*

Brunel *in the start of leg nine.*

his planned course and give chase: he couldn't afford to let *Brasil 1* out of his sight. *Brunel's* Matt Humphries did likewise while *Ericsson* continued to disappear towards the horizon, so much so that it was suggested in jest that skipper Neal McDonald must have decided to head home to England. *Ericsson* paid a big price: when they tacked back along the coast, they fell in behind the rest of the fleet because the wind direction had stayed in favour of those inshore.

It was no surprise in the conditions that *Brasil 1*, carrying the same new light-weather headsail it had used with such impact when it won the previous leg, was leading the pack. What was surprising, however, was the speed of *ABN AMRO ONE*—or lack of it. She was bringing up the rear in conditions that usually suited her. "All day yesterday the boat just didn't feel itself," Sanderson reported. "The conditions should have been great for us. Normally we are a bullet on a good 13-to-15-knot beat. We must have hit something in the water and it has knocked off the fairing between the steel and the carbon fibre part of our keel. The damage is not structural, but it sure is slowing us down. What a huge relief that we don't need a result in this leg to win overall."

Conditions were typical of the region, with a damp fog that limited visibility to around 2 miles. As the yachts pushed north past the coast of Germany and on towards the northern tip of Denmark, the erratic nature of the wind continued to frustrate the navigators and tacticians. Instead of remaining relatively constant in direction, this invisible force was wafting through near 90 degrees in no regular pattern, and if you got a shift wrong then it was very easy to go from being the legendary rooster to the feather duster. At one stage *The Black Pearl* missed one big shift and crashed to last place while *Brasil 1* continued to lead— a situation that theoretically meant the Brazilians had climbed into second place in the overall results . . . but a lot of miles remained to be covered before the finish in Göteborg.

Cayard then had nothing to lose, so he bit the bullet, tacked his yacht, and sailed hard right towards the coast. It was a losing leg, but the coast was where the leaders had found better breeze. At the same time *ABN AMRO ONE* and *Ericsson* elected to stay offshore.

On what was the final night at sea, after 8 months of competition and more than 32,000 nautical miles under sail, a fairytale finish was unfolding.

Clockwise from top left: The Black Pearl rounding the lighthouse Trubaduren a few minutes before ABN AMRO TWO.

Brasil 1 *and* Ericsson *at the start of leg nine from Rotterdam to Göteborg.*

In conditions that didn't suit them, the youngsters aboard *ABN AMRO TWO*, the team that had gone to hell and back on the crossing of the Atlantic, had mastered every tricky wind shift close to Denmark's shoreline and established what appeared to be an unassailable lead. At sunrise they were 15 nautical miles ahead of *Brasil 1,* while *The Black Pearl* had made a remarkable recovery and re-emerged in third place.

Having seen the rises and falls in placings along the way from Rotterdam, and with the forecast indicating light winds, the *ABN AMRO TWO* crew knew they weren't safe. "Once more left drifting around in little or no wind," reported navigator Simon Fisher. "It is a nervous time here on *ABN AMRO TWO* as we ghost through the water at the head of the fleet. We are all praying that we have enough breeze to carry us over the finish. Simeon (Tienpont) is up the rig looking for breeze. At 105 kilos it is no mean feat for us hauling his bulk up the 30-metre mast!"

Try as they did to maintain momentum, the youngsters were soon dealt the cruellest of blows. Just 15 miles from the finish they hit the wall. The gentle breeze that was propelling their boat towards victory took one last gasp and died. It was then a waiting game. Waiting for the breeze to return. While their yacht sat motionless on a glassy sea the crew tried desperately to harness anything that felt like a puff of wind. Meantime, unbeknown to them, the hunters in their wake and beyond the horizon were still carrying good breeze and making 5 knots in the right direction.

"It was like torture," recalled crewman Andy Lewis. "It got worse when someone looked aft and saw a dot on the horizon, then we watched that dot take the shape of a triangle. There was nothing we could do but hope it wasn't a race yacht. The guys were constantly checking it through the binoculars, then someone said 'it's the pirates,' and we knew we were in trouble."

Clockwise from left: ABN AMRO TWO *on leg nine.*

Skipper Paul Cayard catches up on sleep on The Black Pearl *during leg nine.*

Gybing during the final approach to Göteborg on board Brunel.

"We finished last in the first race in Sanxenxo in Spain, and last on the last leg today; but it was what happened in between that mattered."
Mike Sanderson, skipper, *ABN AMRO ONE*

Clockwise from top: Paul Cayard carefully steers The Black Pearl *towards the leg nine finish.*

Brunel *approaches the finish line at Göteborg.*

The Black Pearl *skipper Paul Cayard gives the thumbs up after winning the leg.*

Brasil 1 *skipper Torben Grael spraying champagne after finishing third.*

The Black Pearl remained on a charge, more determined than ever to plunder the prize for the leg. And the breeze ably assisted their mission: it held in strength for them and they were soon able to sail up past their quarry, the still listless leader. Soon, though, it became apparent that the fight wasn't over. The breeze reignited *ABN AMRO TWO* and it began to make a dramatic comeback. It was *The Black Pearl* who was then looking over their shoulders. The youngsters would eventually get back to within 70 yards of the leader but couldn't penetrate further.

Both boats were making 7 knots in 7 knots of breeze on a stunning Swedish summer day, and, as they closed on the coastline, they were joined by more than 5,000 spectator craft. On shore an equally enthusiastic crowd, which Paul Cayard estimated to be 200,000, was there to cheer the yachts into port.

By the time the two yachts entered the channel marking the passage to the finish line under Göteborg's Älvsborg Bridge, the race was over. There were no more passing lanes, and with a mass of spectator boats crammed

between them and their pursuer, *The Black Pearl* was able to surge home the winner by just 4 minutes and 15 seconds. The Pirates of the Caribbean team had finally claimed the position at the top of the podium that they so often threatened to take since they found form in Melbourne.

When Paul Cayard stepped ashore to accept the leg winner's trophy from the patron of the Volvo Ocean Race, Sweden's Prince Carl Phillip, he relived his best memories of the race for the waiting media and the thousands of people cramming the dock, then announced his retirement from round-the-world racing. Cayard said that filling second place this time was almost as satisfying as being the outright winner 8 years earlier, and the time had come to stay ashore . . . but he might consider managing a syndicate in the future.

There was an equally rousing welcome awaiting *ABN AMRO TWO* and then *Brasil 1* when they crossed the line in third spot. *Brunel* was fourth, its best result in the entire race, and *Ericsson* fifth home. But the best was

literally saved for last. The outright winner of the Volvo Ocean Race, *ABN AMRO ONE*, sailed into port to receive the massively boisterous and noisy welcome it deserved.

At the dock and after accepting the crystal Fighting Finish winner's trophy from Prince Carl Phillip, Mike Sanderson summed up the situation perfectly: "We finished last in the first race in Sanxenxo in Spain, and last on the last leg today: but it was what happened in between that mattered."

Leg 9 Results

Leg Position	Yacht	Elapsed Time	Leg Points	Rotterdam In-Port Race Points	Previous Points	Overall Points	Overall Standing
1	The Black Pearl	2d 2h 44m	7.0	2.5	63.5	73.0	2
2	ABN AMRO TWO	2d 2h 48m	6.0	1.0	51.5	58.5	4
3	Brasil 1	2d 3h 32m	5.0	3.0	59.0	67.0	3
4	Brunel	2d 4h 26m	4.0	1.5	10.0	15.5	7
5	Ericsson	2d 5h 10m	3.0	2.0	50.0	55.0	5
6	ABN AMRO ONE	2d 5h 26m	2.0	3.5	90.5	96.0	1
7	movistar	did not race	0	0.0	48.0	48.0	6

The scene was in a centuries-old, typically English pub that, to this day, nestles right on the waterfront at the harbour entrance in "Old Portsmouth." It was 1971, and among the crowd enjoying the warm ambiance of the heavily timbered, smoke-filled bar were Colonel Bill Whitbread, of the famous brewing family, and Admiral Otto Steiner, of the Royal Naval Sailing Association. They were socialising over a few pints of beer and their primary topic of conversation just happened to be ocean yacht racing.

Times Gone

By

Before they walked out of the bar, a seed of an idea had germinated, and, in a short period of time, it had grown to where an incredible adventure, The Whitbread Round The World Race, was announced.

There is no way that Whitbread or Steiner could have even remotely envisaged what would come as a consequence of them having those few beers and a chat. The world of international sailing has a lot to thank them for.

When the inaugural race started off Plymouth on September 8, 1973 it was thought that it might be staged just once. It attracted 17 yachts representing 6 nations, and 167 adventurous and courageous sailors. They were faced with a perilous, 27,000-nautical-mile passage around the planet where they would experience everything that the forces of nature could deliver. For some sailors, the race was like being banished to the end of the earth, and they were. Until then fewer than 10 privately owned yachts had rounded the world's southernmost and most dangerous point of land—Cape Horn.

Danger stalked the contest from start to finish; so much so that by the time the circumnavigation was complete three sailors had perished as a consequence of howling gales and murderous seas. Not surprisingly, there were calls from some quarters for any thoughts of future races to be abandoned. But the spirit of adventure, and a desire to push human endeavour to a new extreme, won through.

The Whitbread/Volvo Ocean Race has been staged every 4 years since its inception. In the 9 races to date, 121 yachts and more than 1,500 men and women have faced this incredible challenge.

Today, what is now the Volvo Ocean Race Round the World is at the pinnacle of extreme sports. Few would argue that a greater test of man and machine could be conceived.

The memories of the sailors are too valuable to be lost, so here a competitor from each of the eight previous events shares their race with us . . .

Englishman **Butch Dalrymple-Smith** was a crewmember aboard the Mexican entry *Sayula II*, the winner of the inaugural Whitbread Round The World Race, which was to later become the Volvo Ocean Race. Prior to competing, he represented England in the Admiral's Cup and Southern Cross Cup ocean racing team championships and was a member of the crew of the Australian yacht *Stormy Petrel*, winner of the One Ton Cup in 1971.

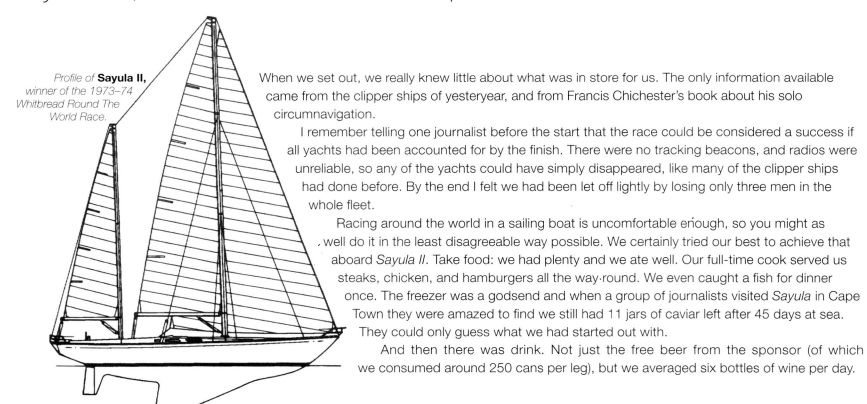

*Profile of **Sayula II**, winner of the 1973–74 Whitbread Round The World Race.*

When we set out, we really knew little about what was in store for us. The only information available came from the clipper ships of yesteryear, and from Francis Chichester's book about his solo circumnavigation.

I remember telling one journalist before the start that the race could be considered a success if all yachts had been accounted for by the finish. There were no tracking beacons, and radios were unreliable, so any of the yachts could have simply disappeared, like many of the clipper ships had done before. By the end I felt we had been let off lightly by losing only three men in the whole fleet.

Racing around the world in a sailing boat is uncomfortable enough, so you might as well do it in the least disagreeable way possible. We certainly tried our best to achieve that aboard *Sayula II*. Take food: we had plenty and we ate well. Our full-time cook served us steaks, chicken, and hamburgers all the way·round. We even caught a fish for dinner once. The freezer was a godsend and when a group of journalists visited *Sayula* in Cape Town they were amazed to find we still had 11 jars of caviar left after 45 days at sea. They could only guess what we had started out with.

And then there was drink. Not just the free beer from the sponsor (of which we consumed around 250 cans per leg), but we averaged six bottles of wine per day.

Masts fell, boats capsized, and men died, and somehow a production yacht with a motley crew managed to win the only round-the-world race that people could sail like gentlemen.

Spirits also went down well. After each day's 6-hour watch those coming off the deck would be handed a rum tonic or a vodka or gin as they stepped down the companionway.

Our watch system was special, with 4 hours on, 4 hours off by night and a 6-hour stint during the day. That way we got enough sleep and a chance to read, write letters, or wash our clothes. There were 12 of us on board, with the owner and the cook working at their own rhythm and two watches of five. By running the boat with four on deck, each of the sailing crew could get 1 day off in every 5. The day off was spent helping with sail changes, washing up, serving the cocktails, and doing a 'special duty,' like repairing sails or topping up the batteries—but it really felt like a break.

We couldn't communicate much and we were all blissfully free of responsibilities to sponsors. *Sayula* only finished two legs with a working radio, and thankfully the organisers were not alarmed by our silences. Although we could rarely participate, there was a daily radio sked among the competitors. We called it 'Children's Hour.' It was mainly monopolised by other crews boringly complaining about how little fun they were having, but the medical problems radioed in to Dr. Robin Leach on *Second Life* were worth a few giggles.

Some boats had their share of personal dramas: at least three boats had mutinies, usually in the form of a refusal to go on deck or a refusal to stay below and cook. On an Italian boat a crewmember had to be disarmed as he threatened the skipper with a knife. And on *Burton Cutter* the paying members of the crew refused to wash up, thinking it should be done by those being paid or at least going for free.

By today's standards, navigation was difficult using a sextant. There were times when we would go weeks without a decent fix, but that never really concerned us. The weather was all ours. There were no weather maps, no outside routers, no satellite photos: just our barograph and a look at the sky and the sea.

Our central heating was wonderful in the Southern Ocean: being able to step below into a warm cosy glow was special. Our only mistake was having the thermostat mounted too close to the companionway entry, so every time the hatch was opened a blast of cold air caused the thermostat to fire up the boiler, turning the interior into a sauna. Later, the unit got swamped when we capsized. Sadly the damage was terminal: the central heating never worked again.

In 1973 watermakers had yet to be invented, so we had to carry enough fresh water to last until the next stopover. *Sayula's* owner monitored consumption carefully and when our parsimony meant we were carrying more than enough, we had the much-appreciated luxury of a shower in hot, fresh water!

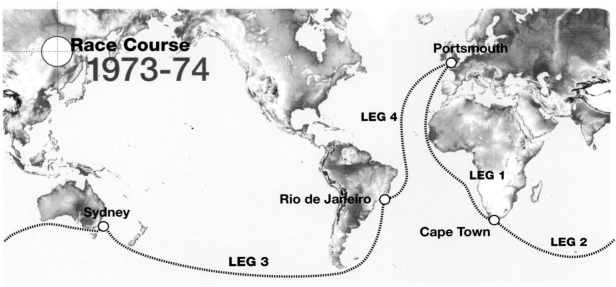

Race Course
1973-74

Portsmouth

LEG 4

LEG 1

Rio de Janeiro

Sydney

Cape Town

LEG 2

LEG 3

A group of journalists that visited *Sayula* in Cape Town were amazed to find we still had 11 jars of caviar left after 45 days at sea. They could only guess what we had started out with. And then there was the drink.

A private bunk in a private cabin with a door to shut out the world: racing has progressed a lot since then, but for the better? We hot bunked of course, but everyone had the peace of his own little corner. We little realised that later participants would only dream of what we took for granted.

Memory is selective. I've almost forgotten how cold it was. How wet we became as our 1970s foul-weather gear failed to keep out the water that gives even today's gear a bit of a struggle. There is an enormous divide between the PVC and wool we used then, and the Gore-Tex and composite piles they use today. But I easily remember those evenings when Quique quietly strummed his guitar (how many Volvo Open 70s took a guitar with them?) and sang soft Mexican folk songs as the sun went down, while we enjoyed cocktails and the yacht glided serenely on through the wine dark sea.

Beneath the languid luxury that this may conjure, we were nevertheless racing. Half of the crew may have been the owner's family, but the rest of us were dedicated boat racers with match racing, world championship, and offshore race wins on our various CVs. Unlike the other boats that excitedly boasted of the speed they reached, we were never satisfied with how fast we were going. In fact in one 3-day period our log recorded no less than 150 sail changes. If we couldn't go fast, at least we tried to avoid going slowly.

Although *Sayula* was well built and survived the rigours of the race rather better than the others, she only just made it—the standing rigging was in tatters by the end. We approached the finish line off Portsmouth on Easter Day with tens of thousands of people on Southsea Beach watching us come in, the tide sweeping us towards the finish. Finally, when we were certain of winning, I asked the owner, Ramon Carlin, if he would allow me to over-crank a runner and bring the mast down. That way we would finish sideways with the rig over the side, make headlines all over the world, and give the spectators something to tell their grandchildren. He actually thought about it for a long time before reluctantly saying 'No . . . because the yacht is not insured.'

On *Sayula* we were fortunate to strike a happy compromise between the pure adventurers, whose pioneering spirit was not matched by their expertise in sailing, and others who were gung-ho racing crews without the hardware to stand the pace. Masts fell, boats capsized, and men died, and somehow a production yacht with a motley crew managed to win the only round-the-world race that people could sail like gentlemen.

1973–74 Results

Position	Yacht	Nationality	Skipper(s)	Corrected Time [days / hours]*
1	Sayula II	Mexico	Ramon Carlin	133d 13h
2	Adventure	Netherlands	Patrick Bryans, Malcolm Skene, George Vallings, Roy Mullender	135d 8h
3	Grand Louis	France	André Viant	138d 15h
4	Kriter	France	Jack Grout, Michael Malinovsky, Alain Gliksman	141d 2h
5	Guia	Italy	Giorgio Falck	142d 19h
6	Great Britain II	United Kingdom	Chay Blyth	144d 11h
7	Second Life	United Kingdom	Roddy Ainslie	150d 8h
8	CSeRB	Italy	Doi Malingri	156d 22h
9	British Soldier	United Kingdom	James Myatt	156d 21h
10	Tauranga	Italy	Eric Pascoli	156d 22h
11	Copernicus	Poland	Zygfryd Perlicki	166d 19h
12	33 Export	France	Jean-Pierre Millet, Dominique Guillet	175d 22h
13	Otago	Poland	Zdzislaw Pienkawa	178d 9h
14	Peter von Danzig	Germany	Reinhard Laucht	179d 15h

5 BOATS DID NOT FINISH THE RACE: *Pen Duick VI*, France; *Burton Cutter*, United Kingdom; *Jakaranda*, South Africa; *Concorde*, France; and *Pen Duick III*, France.

*corrected time takes the handicap into account

Race Two 1977–78

After a successful career in dinghy sailing, Switzerland's **Pierre Fehlmann** entered the world of ocean racing later in life than most, but when he did, he certainly left his mark, especially on The Whitbread Race. In five contests he never finished worse than fourth. In his third Whitbread, in 1985–86, he scored the fastest overall time with the maxi, *UBS Switzerland*. His first race was in 1977–78 and here he tells that story.

PPL PHOTO AGENCY

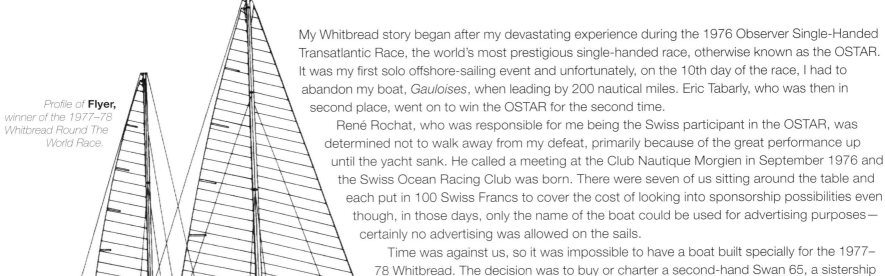

Profile of **Flyer,** *winner of the 1977–78 Whitbread Round The World Race.*

My Whitbread story began after my devastating experience during the 1976 Observer Single-Handed Transatlantic Race, the world's most prestigious single-handed race, otherwise known as the OSTAR. It was my first solo offshore-sailing event and unfortunately, on the 10th day of the race, I had to abandon my boat, *Gauloises*, when leading by 200 nautical miles. Eric Tabarly, who was then in second place, went on to win the OSTAR for the second time.

René Rochat, who was responsible for me being the Swiss participant in the OSTAR, was determined not to walk away from my defeat, primarily because of the great performance up until the yacht sank. He called a meeting at the Club Nautique Morgien in September 1976 and the Swiss Ocean Racing Club was born. There were seven of us sitting around the table and each put in 100 Swiss Francs to cover the cost of looking into sponsorship possibilities even though, in those days, only the name of the boat could be used for advertising purposes — certainly no advertising was allowed on the sails.

Time was against us, so it was impossible to have a boat built specially for the 1977–78 Whitbread. The decision was to buy or charter a second-hand Swan 65, a sistership to *Sayula II,* the winner of the first Whitbread race in 1973–74.

By February 1977, 6 months before the start of the race, we had found our main sponsor, chartered a Swan 65 built in 1973, ordered the sails, and started the recruitment of an all-Swiss crew. I was of the opinion that to run a big boat campaign it was better to recruit good dinghy skippers rather than good crewmembers from larger boats. It is easier to train

Just after passing the equator on the first leg, the generator and main motor used as back up both gave up on us, and as a result we lost all further contact with land.

good sailors with no offshore experience than it is to bring aboard sailors who already have offshore racing experience and are set in their ways when it comes to helming and general rules.

The criteria used for the selection of the crew from among 200 candidates spanned a five-page questionnaire that referred to:

1) Results obtained in previous dinghy races
2) Professional training
3) Ability to become part of commando-type team

The final selection of 20 potential crewmembers was based on the response to the questionnaire and a personal interview. This was carried out over 2 long weekends using my father's Corona 35. Three days of sailing a 35-foot yacht with a 10-man crew in quite tough weather conditions enabled me to get a reasonably accurate judgment about an individual's character.

The Swan 65 was available from the end of April in the Caribbean, which gave us only 2 months to prepare the boat and train the team, none of whom had ever sailed on anything like a yacht that large. A few had raced One-Tonners, but most had sailed only dinghies.

Our budget was very tight and, as a result, we had only one suit of sails for the whole race. I had organised a fan club for each crewmember as each had to buy their individual kits of oilskins and safety harnesses and, in

Disque d'Or skippered by Pierre Fehlmann.

PPL PHOTO AGENCY

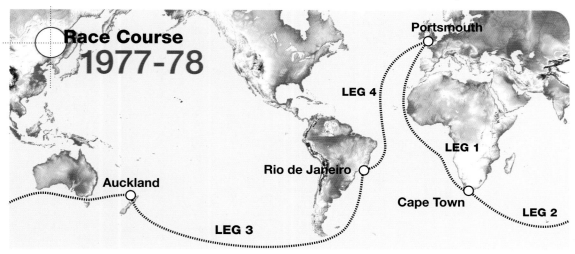

Race Course 1977-78

Portsmouth

LEG 4

Rio de Janeiro

Auckland

LEG 3

Cape Town

LEG 1

LEG 2

addition, pay 3,000 Swiss Francs to the SORC. This deposit was paid back as 500 Swiss francs after each leg and 1,000 Swiss Francs at the finish, a plan that meant it was less likely that they would have to go begging on each port of call!

The Swan 65 was christened *Disque d'Or* and was prepared in Swanwick, England, by the team members themselves. Over two periods, in the lead-up to the race, they were trained in the handling of the boat and how to maintain it.

As part of our preparation I did a lot of analysis of different sail configurations. It involved statistical work where we tested the speed of the boat against the wind speed and angle every 10 seconds over a 10-minute period. My overall plan was to race offshore with the same level of concentration an Olympic team would give to a race over a short triangular course, but with one big difference—our first leg was going to last 42 days.

As I was the only one on the team who had had any astronomical or radio-communication training, we hired Olivier Stern Veyrin for the first leg to Cape Town. He had sailed in the first Whitbread on *33 Export* and by being with us he was able to train Hans Bernhard, our navigator, in the secrets of the sextant and the stars.

At this time there were no Sat Navs, weather decoders, or navigation software. We didn't receive full, inter-connected data for wind speed, angle, and direction, and we used a propeller log with a winding shaft to measure the distance we had travelled. Our average course was always a rough estimate made by those on deck.

Fifteen yachts between 50 feet and 78 feet took their place on the start line off Portsmouth: Two of the starters had been built specially for this race and the only result was on corrected time, something that I didn't believe was fair, since the first boats arrived 10 to 15 days before the last, and had therefore been sailing in totally different wind conditions.

As far as food was concerned, it was all quite a normal affair. *Disque d'Or* was a cruising yacht, so it had a huge freezer on board. That meant we were able to have meat three times a week, with other meals based mainly on pasta and some pre-cooked products that we made up as and when we needed them. We took 1.2 litres of water per crewmember per day for each leg, so thunderstorms were always very welcome, because we could fill up our tanks.

Our much-needed weather information back then came only via Morse code. Nobody on board could translate the transmission at normal speed, but fortunately we had found a decoder, so when the signal was accurate and without too much interference, we were able to print the information that had been transmitted. We recorded the messages at a certain time each day, and if the reception wasn't too clear we would pass it through the decoder several times to get the information.

We then had to plot on the map the locations of the low- and high-pressure systems, what pressure they were, and what fronts were moving in. This job meant nearly 2 hours of work for the navigator, and even then we still had only a very vague idea of how the weather systems were unfolding. These maps were only ever available for the Atlantic, and were plotted on the basis of readings made by cargo ships that were transmitting air pressure and cloud cover information to different meteorological centres.

Just after passing the equator on the first leg, the generator and main motor used as backup both gave up on us, and, as a result, we lost all further contact with land (at that time there was no such thing as a beacon or automatic GPS system).

We arrived in Cape Town at around 2300 on a Friday evening with nobody to meet us, simply because no one knew we were coming—and because at this time in history, the hand-held VHF was a mere project on somebody's desk somewhere in the world. We had finished the first leg without even enough electrical current on board to make our electronics systems work, and this had made it impossible for us to advise the race committee, who were on watch 24 hours a day at one end of the bridge jetty in Cape Town.

This might have been the second Whitbread Round The World Race, but for us it was always a total unknown. Our passion for winning and understanding the race meant we finished fourth overall—a result we were very pleased with, especially considering we were a team that had never stepped on board a large offshore yacht before we began our pre-race training sessions.

We finished in 142 days and 10 hours, a time that was 11 days, 3 hours better than our sistership *Sayula's* winning time in the previous race.

1977–78 Results

Position	Yacht	Nationality	Skipper(s)	Corrected Time* [days / hours]
1	Flyer	Netherlands	Cornelis van Rietschoten	119d 1h
2	King's Legend	United Kingdom	Nick Ratcliffe, Mike Clancy	121d 11h
3	Traité de Rome	EEC	Philippe Hanin	121d 18h
4	Disque d'Or	Switzerland	Pierre Fehlmann	122d 10h
5	ADC Accutrac	United Kingdom	Clare Francis	126d 20h
6	Gauloises II	France	Eric Loizeau	127d 7h
7	Adventure	United Kingdom	James Watts, David Leslie, Ian Bailey-Willmot, Robin Duchesne	128d 2h
8	Neptune	France	Bernard Deguy	130d 11h
9	B&B Italia	Italy	Corrado di Majo	132d 2h
10	33 Export	France	Alain Gabbay (31 min)	133d 00h
11	Tielsa	Netherlands	Dirk Nauta (36 min)	133d 00h
12	Great Britain II	United Kingdom	Rob James	134d 10h
13	Debenhams	United Kingdom	John Ridgway	135d 19h
14	Japy-Hermes	France	Jean Michel Viant	143d 6h
15	Heath's Condor	United Kingdom	Leslie Williams, Robin Knox-Johnston	144d 00h

*corrected time takes the handicap into account

RaceThree 1981–82

The 1981–82 Whitbread Race was Englishman **Les Williams'** third attempt to win. He raced on *FCF Challenger* in a contest that was full of surprises, the most startling of which came at the end of the first leg into Cape Town. The Italian entry, *Vivanapoli*, arrived in port 8 days behind the others with the crew having an amazing explanation as to why they were so slow. They had been stopped by an Angolan gunboat and boarded, and when the Angolans discovered South Africans in the crew, they arrested them as spies. It took the Italian embassy a week to arrange their release.

Profile of **Flyer,** *winner of the 1981–82 Whitbread Round The World Race.*

Having learned from my experiences in skippering in the first two Whitbread Races, I started preparations for my third attempt in good time. I commissioned the design of a GRP 80-footer from David Alan-Williams, who had sailed with me in two previous races with Peter Blake as his watch leader.

The project was going to schedule—until the boat-building yard was taken over by an ex-employee who wanted to get out of my contract, and then the management at the UK office of our American-based sponsor also took a dislike to the deal.

It was all starting to unravel. I should have given up there and then, but I was too stubborn. As a consequence I finished up with a poorly built yacht and a sponsor who would walk away. In the end, my only option was to find paying crew to fund the actual cost of getting the boat around the world.

We started the race from Portsmouth with a motley crew and a yacht heavily laden with several tons of food because we couldn't afford to ship it to forward ports of call. Our small budget also saw us having an inferior sail wardrobe, particularly when it came to light weather sails.

Flyer, the race favourite, led the fleet away from the start while we maintained a good position close behind until the Doldrums, where we began to suffer from our lack of light weather sails and the extra weight we were carrying. Once clear of the Doldrums, we caught up dramatically and were due to finish only a few hours behind *Flyer* into Cape Town, until fate struck again and we were totally becalmed for 36 hours. Five other yachts then passed us and led us to the line. I blasphemed!

There were plenty of repairs to be done in Cape Town, but we had no money to pay for them. Our saviour was a former Royal Navy friend who lived locally. He was able to find a yard that could do the work at the right price, then he organised some day charters for the boat so we could raise funds to cover the expenses of the next leg.

The crew had a great time in Cape Town—some too great a time. My most experienced watch leader fell madly in love with an unusual local girl and decided to marry her, and there was nothing his mates or I could do to dissuade him. He stayed there and got married, apparently much to his regret some time later.

For me it was a relief to get to sea again. David Alan-Williams had joined us for this leg, as he wanted to prove the boat he had designed. As the Southern Ocean winds increased we pushed hard and put in some startling 24-hour runs. Unfortunately, this effort saw us damage almost every sail we carried, and then a catastrophe came when the boom snapped as a result of a disgraceful piece of engineering. We made an emergency repair and managed to arrive off the coast of New Zealand in third place behind *Flyer* and *Ceramco NZ*, only to find a windless hole again and have five yachts come from behind and beat us into Auckland. I began to think I should not have blasphemed off Cape Town, but I fear I did it again.

The Kiwi hospitality helped us to survive our poor results and prepare for the next leg round Cape Horn. We needed fresh food, fruit and vegetables, and this led to us being introduced to a keen local sailor, a farmer who bred

beef cattle: 'Take me to Argentina with you and I'll kill and chill a cow for you and provide the fresh stuff you'll need,' he told us. He was a big, powerful, fit man, and we needed to eat, so we had all the meat we needed in Auckland for the next leg. He turned out to be great crewmember and a wonderful character.

We led the fleet at the end of the first day out of Auckland with *Flyer* close astern, but slipped back in the lighter winds overnight and were probably a mile behind the leader in the morning. When it came to weather forecasting I had to rely on the barometer and my own guess, as I had not been able to afford a weatherfax, so knowing I could not out-sail *Flyer* and *Ceramco*, I had to take a 'flyer' of my own if I was to get a result. That brought about a moment of madness: I tacked away from the fleet and headed south. As it turned out, the move was absolute stupidity because we sailed into light winds while the rest of the fleet sped on. We rounded the Horn at the back of the fleet, but in good old naval fashion, we celebrated the rounding by splicing the main brace with Pusser's Rum. It was a pleasant passage north from there. We sailed inside the Falkland Islands and started to catch up to a few of the slower boats, but were never going to be in the results. All I wanted to do by then was get to the finish.

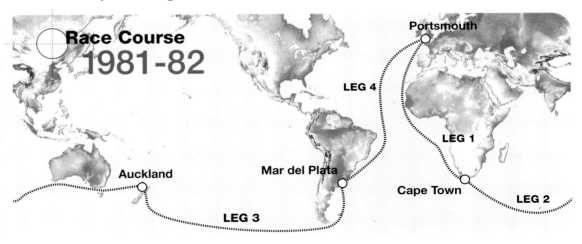

Race Course
1981-82

Portsmouth

LEG 4

LEG 1

Auckland

Mar del Plata

Cape Town

LEG 2

LEG 3

Mar del Plata was a wonderful place, and it was made even better when my wife arrived there with the news that the chairman for the Co-op Bank had been changed and the new man wanted to re-activate the sponsorship for the leg home to England. The boat was to be re-named *First Co-Operative* and he had arranged for the British Ambassador to travel, with his wife, from Buenos Aires, so she could perform the ceremony. My wife had been asked to help organise the whole affair for the bank before the chairman and his team flew in from England. With money coming our way, the new name was duly applied to the yacht and refreshments were arranged from the Yacht Club. We then awaited the big day.

1981–82 Results

Position	Yacht	Nationality	Skipper(s)	Corrected Time* [days / hours]
1	Flyer	Netherlands	Cornelis van Rietschoten	119d 1h
2	Charles Heidsieck III	France	Alain Gabbay	120d 7h
3	Kriter XI	France	Andre Viant	120d 10h
4	Disque d'Or III	Switzerland	Pierre Fehlmann	123d 11h
5	Outward Bound	New Zealand	Digby Taylor	124d 11h
6	Xargo III	South Africa	Padda Kuttel	124d 19h
7	Mor bihan	France	Phillipe Poupon	125d 15h
8	Berge Viking	Norway	Peder Lunde	125d 16h
9	Alaska Eagle	United States	Skip Novak, Neil Bergt	126d 10h
10	Euromarche	France	Eric Tabarly	126d 23h
11	Ceramco NZ	New Zealand	Peter Blake	127d 17h
12	Skopbank of Finland	Finland	Kenneth Gahmberg	128d 15h
13	RollyGo	Italy	Giorgio Falck	129d 20h
14	Traité de Rome	EEC	Antonio Chioatto	130d 23h
15	Croky	Belgium	Gustaaf Versluys	133d 23h
16	FCF Challenger	United Kingdom	Leslie Williams	138d 15h
17	United Friendly	United Kingdom	Chay Blyth	141d 10h
18	Walross III Berlin	Germany	Jean-Michel Viant	143d 19h
19	Licor 43	Spain	Joaquin Coello	160d 2h
20	Ilgagomma	Italy	Roberto Vianello	160d 9h

9 BOATS DID NOT FINISH THE RACE: *European Uni.*, Belgium; *33 Export*, France; *Gauloises III*, France; *La Barca Laboratorio*, Italy; *Save Venice*, Italy; *Vivanapoli*, Italy; *Scandanavian*, Sweden; *Swedish Entry*, Sweden; *Bubblegum*, United Kingdom. **corrected time takes the handicap into account*

HMS Endurance, the Antarctic watchdog, was in port at the time and her skipper, Captain Nick Barker, was an old friend from naval sailing. We met for drinks most days and were invited to the Argentine Navy Petty Officers' Mess. Most of the Argentines spoke good English and one day, to my surprise, they announced, "Soon we go the Malvinas." I knew Malvinas was their name for the Falklands, so I said 'But the Malvinas are British.'

"Yes, we know that," was the reply, "but you don't want them anymore so we are moving in." They actually gave me a date some weeks ahead, and I laughed and said they were joking, but they assured me they were not. Soon after, this same statement was confirmed to Nick by his own Petty Officers.

The renaming duly took place with proper ceremony and after the ceremony we were invited aboard *Endurance,* and it was there that we told the Ambassador of the planned Argentine invasion of the Falklands, but still there was little reaction. In the end we were proved right: the invasion took place soon after we had sailed, and Britain declared it was "surprised and shocked" by the move.

Things were looking good prior to our departure—until I was called to the Yacht Club and asked to pay some bills. Apparently, the Co-op Bank boss had neglected to settle the bill for the meal he'd invited my wife and me to, and also the bills associated with the re-naming of the boat hadn't been paid. I had to pay it all from my own account so we could start with the rest of the fleet. It appears that the money was eventually sent, but by that time the war had started and the cash just disappeared into Argentine coffers.

It was wonderful to have a boat at normal weight for this leg. We led from the start and by nightfall *Flyer* and *Ceramco* were barely visible on the horizon astern. What a difference, until the wind fell light in the Doldrums and the others passed us.

I felt we could catch the others once clear of the light winds, but then disaster struck. I was off watch and in my bunk when suddenly the boat came upright and all went quiet. I knew the mast was gone. It had simply disintegrated, the longest piece left being no more than 6 feet in length. We were still 1,000 miles from home, but within a couple of hours we had set a jury rig using the spinnaker poles as a bipod mainmast and the boom as a mizzen. We cut up what was left of the genoa and mainsail and we were off to windward again. Ours was the 10th dismasting in the race. Chay Blyth caught up with us 2 days later and passed us a bottle of whisky as consolation.

Flyer was first to finish in Portsmouth and *Ceramco* second. We were the fifth yacht home, a result I was proud of considering our unique rig.

RICK TOMLINSON

The 1985 race was to be third time lucky for me. My first Whitbread was in the 1977–78 race on *King's Legend*. Your first is always the best as it's grand adventure. I navigated with a sextant and a lot of guesswork and we broke enough gear and sails en route to fill a container. Along this wake of disaster we had little or no communication with the shore or other boats, which never bothered anyone as we didn't know any better. **Skip Novak**

Race Four 1985–86

*Profile of **L'Esprit d'Equipe,** winner of the 1985–86 Whitbread Round The World Race.*

In 1981, our original project went belly up when our mysterious Austrian owner did a runner from several banks in Europe just before the boat was due to be launched. It never left the shipyard, and in the wake of this fiasco, I was quickly headhunted by the California-based *Alaska Eagle* project. That race was another learning experience, but regardless, when it was over I was truly a Whitbread addict—and, make no mistake, it is an addiction.

With some exceptions, projects during the eighties were still owner driven, possibly with some light sponsorship attached to give it credibility—unless you were at the right place at the right time, à la Peter Blake in New Zealand, or had the business savvy and connections of a Pierre Fehlmann.

The pattern of strange circumstances in my sailing career combined again in 1985 and I found myself in charge of the maxi *Drum*, owned by rock star Simon Le Bon, of Duran Duran, and his two managers, Mike and Paul Berrow. *Drum* started life as the unfinished hull of *Colt Cars*, a design commissioned from Ron Holland by Rob James, who had sadly passed away during its construction. We held the notion that we were in with a chance because Blake had commissioned the same design, and we had assembled a crack crew of professional deep-water men.

The drama of the keel falling off *Drum* and the yacht capsizing during the Fastnet Race, and our miraculous recovery to be on the Whitbread start line just weeks later, are well documented. Before that disaster, we already had a shock during an inshore race at

Cowes Week when *Portatan*, later renamed *Atlantic Privateer*, and one of the new Farr designs, just walked away from us as if we were standing still.

This was the beginning of the Farr revolution that dominated The Whitbread throughout two more races and continued with the Volvo Ocean 60s. Unlike today, when the boats are built into a box rule and virtually all look alike to the dockside punter, the IOR encouraged design and scaling theories at both ends of the spectrum and usually well before the event, but when it was all too late to change, the writing was on the wall.

So we started the fourth running of The Whitbread knowing, that without serious damage to the Farr boats, we would be struggling not to embarrass ourselves, let alone win a leg or two. The psychological implications of this were profound, but there was nothing to do but grin and bear it and get on with the racing. Remarkably, our moment of glory came early when we led the fleet out of the Solent — but it was downhill from there.

The Whitbread was a simple circumnavigation back then and leg one to Cape Town was always the most significant. After crashing into the fresh headwinds of the southeast trades below the equator, only two of the seven

RICK TOMLINSON

boats in the maxi class arrived in Cape Town unscathed. The rest of us lost rigs, suffered hull delamination, or had keels move, and that put days between us and the leaders, *UBS* and *Lion New Zealand*.

The standards of comfort on board most boats in the 1985–86 race had evolved to a certain degree of spartan living, with an open plan layout below and not much protection on deck. Other things had also changed from the previous race. Gone was the booze supply, ditto the freezer full with roasts and other luxuries. But the cook was retained on most boats, even though some on board claimed ours was a waste of space as anyone could mix up a freeze-dried mess as badly as he could. Privacy was afforded in partitioned cubicles rather than cabins, but we at least had a head with three walls and a door on it. Shifting to the windward side after a tack during the off-watch was done enthusiastically by some and roundly resented by others.

I view the 1985–86 Whitbread as being a watershed race because of the fact that very few crews, other than the principals, were being paid. It would change for future races, but back then most crew were just budding professionals having a hard time getting to the paycheck level in the sport. For this reason I think those early events were a lot tougher on crews in a psychological sense.

Sailing aboard Drum during the 1985–86 Whitbread Round The World Race.

Race Course
1985-86

Portsmouth

LEG 4

LEG 1

Auckland

Punta del Este

Cape Town

LEG 2

LEG 3

These were also the days before shore support crew. Once the crew landed in port, the next day was spent de-rigging, and then a full schedule of repairs and rebuilding was meted out. Rather than the masseuse, we had the toolbox, instead of the shore-side "psychologist" of today, we were kept on the straight by using a long-board for 8 hours fairing the hull. There were no cooks and bottle washers—we took our meals in the pub, out of our own pocket. Spending time with your press officer, or flying home to the family between legs, as some crews do today, was unheard of. And email? Well, if Mom was lucky she got a postcard or two.

On arrival in Cape Town it was discovered that *Drum* had almost lost its keel again, so we set about rebuilding the boat prior to the more demanding second leg through the Southern Ocean to Auckland. It was a credit to our crew during this period that we only lost one man to the dock. He thought better about lunging out into the Southern Ocean on what was a highly suspect, untested platform that was again being denigrated in the press. Ron Holland's brother, Phil, was the replacement. On joining the crew the New Zealander told his mother, 'Mama, good news is that I am coming home. Bad news is that I'm coming on *Drum*!'

Although enormous pressures to perform—more or less in line with the compensation packages—clearly exist now, back in 1985 we laboured under the same stress. But these stresses were not dealt with in an intelligent fashion. They manifested themselves in weird and wonderful ways by the crews while at sea, but in port the stresses led to incidents that would be unthinkable today.

1985–86 Results

Position	Yacht	Nationality	Skipper(s)	Corrected Time* [days / hours]
1	L'Esprit d'Equipe	Lionel Péan	111d 23h	
2	Philips Innovator	Netherlands	Dirk Nauta	112d 21h
3	Fazer Finland	Finland	Michael Berner	115d 00h
4	UBS Switzerland	Switzerland	Pierre Fehlmann	117d 4h
5	Rucanor Tristar	Belgium	Gustaf Versluys, Ann Lippens	118d 9h
6	Fortuna Lights	Spain	Javier Visiers, Jorgie Brufau, Antonio Guiu	121d 00h
7	Lion New Zealand	New Zealand	Peter Blake	121d 7h
8	Drum	United Kingdom	Skip Novak	122d 6h
9	Equity & Law	Netherlands	Pleun van der Lugt	123d 6h
10	Cote d'Or	Belgium	Eric Tabarly	125d 19h
11	Shadow of Switzerland	Switzerland	Otto & Nora Zehender-Mueller	128d 11h
12	Norsk Data GB	United Kingdom	Bob Salmon	136d 1h
13	SAS Baia Viking	Denmark	Jesper Norsk	144d 18h

2 BOATS DID NOT FINISH THE RACE: *NZI Enterprise,* New Zealand; and *Atlantic Privateer,* United States.

**corrected time takes the handicap into account

I vividly recall the time the crew of *Privateer* arrived at our *Drum* party in the Hamble dressed as members of the Ku Klux Klan. Other in-port incidents included the spectacular fist fight between Bongers (*Privateer*) and Simon Gundry (*Lion*) in the bar at the Royal Cape Yacht Club over a minor disagreement, crew disappearing for days and weeks into the hinterland with a willing victim, wrecked cars, bail bonds, and the vicarious pleasure of Simon Le Bon's teenage fans. These all gave colour to what was a classic voyage around the world.

It is of course slightly apocryphal, but not far off the mark, when I explain to people where we came from and how we (I mean they) have arrived to the present state of the genre: true racing machines manned by dedicated soldiers of fortune. It was something we had always strived for. To that end in 1985–86 no spirits were allowed (unless you were Eric Tabarly), which was fair enough. In 1989–90 out went the books—too heavy. In 1993–94 music was banned—too much weight and distraction. In 1997–98 one set of clothes and shared sleeping bags, yes sir! And nowadays? Shaved heads are de rigueur, and even talking to each other (other than about boat speed) is verboten!

RICK TOMLINSON

Magnus Olsson celebrates a new top speed aboard Drum *in the Southern Ocean.*

Englishman **Vincent Geake** is considered to be one of the world's best offshore navigators and sailing theorists. In the 1989–90 Whitbread he joined Lawrie Smith as navigator aboard *Rothmans*. That race brought the beginning of the professional era: big name sponsors, big budgets, new expectations on skippers for media support, increased rewards for crews but increased demands as well.

Race Five 1989–90

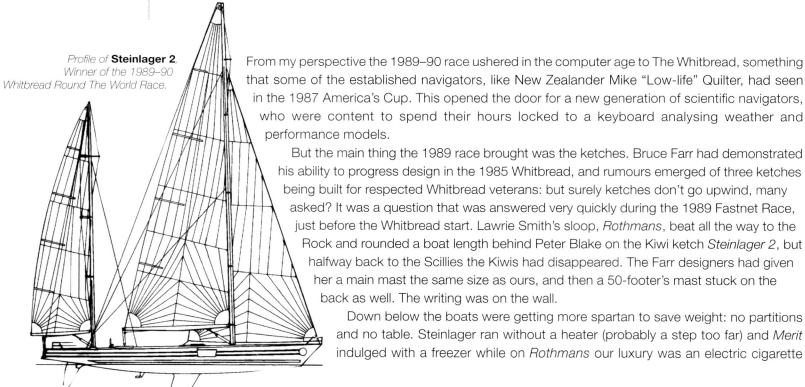

Profile of **Steinlager 2**, *Winner of the 1989–90 Whitbread Round The World Race.*

From my perspective the 1989–90 race ushered in the computer age to The Whitbread, something that some of the established navigators, like New Zealander Mike "Low-life" Quilter, had seen in the 1987 America's Cup. This opened the door for a new generation of scientific navigators, who were content to spend their hours locked to a keyboard analysing weather and performance models.

But the main thing the 1989 race brought was the ketches. Bruce Farr had demonstrated his ability to progress design in the 1985 Whitbread, and rumours emerged of three ketches being built for respected Whitbread veterans: but surely ketches don't go upwind, many asked? It was a question that was answered very quickly during the 1989 Fastnet Race, just before the Whitbread start. Lawrie Smith's sloop, *Rothmans*, beat all the way to the Rock and rounded a boat length behind Peter Blake on the Kiwi ketch *Steinlager 2*, but halfway back to the Scillies the Kiwis had disappeared. The Farr designers had given her a main mast the same size as ours, and then a 50-footer's mast stuck on the back as well. The writing was on the wall.

Down below the boats were getting more spartan to save weight: no partitions and no table. Steinlager ran without a heater (probably a step too far) and *Merit* indulged with a freezer while on *Rothmans* our luxury was an electric cigarette

Every night brought damage, so much that we called the midnight watch 'the carnage watch' or 'the watch that time forgot.' Spinnaker halyards, poles, and booms all broke with monotonous regularity.

KOS

shore crews and the media. This chore fell to the navigator and I could spend a couple of hours shouting down the microphone without success trying to connect Lawrie with Barry Pickthall for his weekly newspaper column. On the second leg of the race, into the Southern Ocean, *Rothmans* pushed south from the rest of the fleet and we were treated to aurora borealis, a spectacular sight, but one that played havoc with our radio propagation. We could still work other boats nearby but could not raise coast stations for a few days. Finally I made contact again through Guam and went back on deck a little shaken: 'Guys, the Berlin Wall has come down'—we had missed the whole excitement of an amazing moment in history.

The nav station was kept warm by the diversity of equipment: an HF weatherfax (plus a spare), weather satellite receiver, Transit satnav, GPS (it cost $20,000 and only received fixes 2 hours per day), Loran, barograph, sailing instruments, radar, VHF and HF radios (plus a spare), battery-charging controls, laptop PC, printer, and the other paraphernalia. By rule we carried a sextant and a set of astro-navigation tables, but I am glad

Lawrie Smith steers Rothmans, *with Vincent Geake standing behind him carrying a chart.*

lighter beside the companionway hatch—the hit from lighting a full round for the seven crew on deck was quite intense. Our efforts to save weight also saw us allowed to carry only the minimum amount of clothing. For the Southern Ocean this meant the socks you were wearing when you walked aboard plus a spare. The first pair were wet very quickly and never dried so people spent days eagerly anticipating the day when they would break out their new socks. For 'Albert' (Neil Graham) that moment came very early one morning, at 3:30 am. He crawled from his bunk to his bag, got out the treasured socks, returned to his bunk and put them on. Luxuriating in the warmth and comfort he then swung out of his bunk and straight into a bucket of water that had been left by someone who was sponging out the bilges. The screams were heard on deck and the miscreant went to ground. He never confessed and we never shopped him, but I can tell you now Albert, 'it was Malcolm!'

Communication was still by HF, juggling between frequency bands and fighting through interminable traffic queues at the coast stations to speak to

Race Course
1989-90

LEG 6

Southampton

Fort Lauderdale

LEG 5

LEG 1

Fremantle

Auckland

Punta del Este

LEG 3

LEG 4

LEG 2

we weren't forced to use them (the spare laptop was accordingly treated with considerably more respect). The navigator was kept from his sleep (not that there was a bunk anyway) by the interminable schedule of all these transmissions, analysing, running course options, and discussing them with Lawrie. It was a fascinating time. The boats trusted deterministic routeing packages like MaxSea using digitised wind fields (no GRIB files then—instead a digitising tablet and do-it-yourself). We created a series of spreadsheet calculators and did our own analysis, developing the VMC concept and sailing fast angles regardless of the compass. Much of the time the crew were simply told 'go as fast as you can somewhere over there.'

We were always pushing hard and the boats did go fast. Several of us closed on a 400-mile day and *Fortuna* broke it. Every night brought damage, so much that we called the midnight watch 'the carnage watch' or 'the watch that time forgot.' Spinnaker halyards, poles, and booms all broke with monotonous regularity. At one point all the booms from one manufacturer were broken—including ours. We carried angle grinders, drills, boxes of hacksaw blades, and pre-drilled repair straps. Spinnaker poles finished legs shorter than they started.

Peter Blake and the Kiwis on *Steinlager 2* dominated the race. They won every leg. Pierre Fehlmann on *Merit* predicted this before we had even crossed the Bay of Biscay on the first leg. He called us on the VHF and said, '*Steinlager's* just passed me going a knot and a half quicker, and she's coming your way!'

Fremantle was the high point of the race: Tracy Edwards won the handicap fleet with her girls arriving in swimwear, and the maxi fleet saw the closest finish ever. After 7,500 miles and 180 degrees of longitude four boats approached Rottnest Island from different directions, all with 100 miles to run but out of sight of each other in the dying Fremantle Doctor (the local sea breeze). We were closing on the reef-strewn island at night when a set of navigation lights suddenly appeared a hundred yards away, and *Merit* crossed tacks behind us. Each time we tacked, *Merit* would follow our line and go an extra boat-length inside us, and Lawrie would scream from on deck 'I've got to go back in again.' Sitting next to me in the nav station Shag Morton (a legend of Whitbread and ocean racing) shrugged his shoulders: the echo-sounder was broken, we had no GPS, and the only information we had was a confused radar echo from the sloping cliffs. He crossed his fingers and said, 'Yes, you can go in again.' On the reach from the island across the stretch of water known as Gage Roads to Fremantle we could not peel headsails because of a broken headfoil, and *Merit* led us round the final turning mark for the run to the finish. Now Lawrie's match-racing skills came through as he lured *Merit* into a gybing duel and threw 23 gybes at them. The boat handling and tactics paid off and *Rothmans* crossed the line 25 seconds ahead after 4 weeks at sea.

1989–90 Results

Position	Yacht	Nationality	Skipper(s)	Corrected Time* [days / hours]
1	Steinlager 2	New Zealand	Peter Blake	128d 9h
2	Fisher & Paykel NZ	New Zealand	Grant Dalton	129d 21h
3	Merit	Switzerland	Pierre Fehlmann	130d 10h
4	Rothmans	United Kingdom	Lawrie Smith	131d 4h
5	The Card	Sweden	Roger Nilson	135d 7h
6	Charles Jourdan	France	Alain Gabbay	136d 15h
7	Fortuna Extra Lights	Spain	Javier de la Gaudera Jan Santana, José Luis Doreste	137d 8h
8	Gatorade	Italy	Giorgio Falck, Hervé Jan Preire Sicouin	138d 14h
9	Union Bank of Finland	Finland	Ludde Ingvall	138d 16h
10	Belmont Finland II	Finland	Harry Harkimo	139d 4h
11	Fazisi	USSR	Alexi Grischenko, Skip Novak, Valeri Alexeev	139d 9h
12	NCB Ireland	Ireland	Joe English	139d 19h
13	British Satquote Defender	United Kingdom	Frank Esson Colin Watkins	143d 12h
14	Equity & Law II	Netherlands	Dirk Nauta	148d 23h
15	Liverpool Enterprise	United Kingdom	Bob Salmon	151d 4h
16	Creightons Naturally	United Kingdom	John Chittendon	162d 6h
17	Esprit de Liberté	France	Patrick Tabarly	164d 21h
18	Maiden	United Kingdom	Tracy Edwards	167d 3h
19	Schlussel von Bremen	Germany	Rolf Renken, Jochen Orgelmann Ham Müeller-Röhlok, Wilhelm Otto-Beck, Peter Weidner	167d 19h
20	With Integrity	United Kingdom	Andy Coghill	170d 16h
21	La Poste	France	Daniel Mallé	181d 22h

2 BOATS DID NOT FINISH THE RACE: *Rucanor Sport,* Belgium; and *Martela OF,* Finland

*corrected time takes the handicap into account

*Profile of **Yamaha,** winner of the Whitbread 60 class of the 1993–94 Whitbread Round The World Race.*

The 1993–94 Whitbread Race was the end of an era—the last year for the maxis and corrected time results. It also heralded the introduction to the race of one-design offshore sailing: the Whitbread 60. **Adrienne Cahalan**

Race Six 1993–94

Fleet start of the Whitbread Race in Fremantle 1994.

This was my first international offshore competition after sailing 18-foot skiffs in Australia and doing local ocean racing as well. The Whitbread had always been my ultimate goal and my chance came when I joined the *US Women's Challenge* just 3 months before the race start. Initially I was a helmsman, but when it became apparent that they needed a navigator, I took over the role. Only a handful of our crew had sailed the race before, so we were very short on experience. It was going to be a big challenge for us to get around the world. Rumours claimed we would not be able to start anyway due to a lack of funds—we had no major sponsor. But we pressed on regardless and got ready to leave at the end of September.

The 1993–94 race was pre-email and internet. Contact with other boats and the shore was made only through a low-speed data-messaging system: Satcom C, using a very simple Apple computer. Still, we were very much on our own when at sea.

Like most others, very few of our crew were paid, and even then it was only a nominal amount. During the stopovers the crews mixed socially, and if you were ever to fly home

We experienced the horror of a mayday from the Italian entry, *Brooksfield*. There was a numb
silence on board our boat for many days as we waited for the report saying that the crew was safe.

during a stopover, you really needed a compelling reason to do so. This was professional yachting in its infancy: the crew worked on their own boats, and if there was a 'shore crew' it consisted at the most of one manager, a sailmaker, and maybe a cook.

During the first leg, *New Zealand Endeavour* dominated the maxi class while Chris Dickson's *Tokio* showed it was the one to beat in the Whitbread 60s. The 60s had also confirmed they could match the maxis for speed. Upon arriving in Uruguay after a first leg of 26 days, it turned out our syndicate did not have the financing to continue. The owners of the boat, Ocean Ventures, cancelled the charter to Nance Frank and her backers, then asked many of the crew, including me, to rejoin the team under the leadership of American Dawn Riley, and subsequently with sponsorship from Heineken.

The second leg from Punta Del Este, Uruguay, to Fremantle was tough—30+ days for most crews in the most remote part of the Southern Ocean, and relatively close to the ice. We were one of the first boats to strike problems, splitting the mainsail in two when we Chinese gybed. We spent 2 days on deck sewing it back together,

128

*Right: Whitbread
60 Heineken
in the 1993–94
Whitbread Round
The World Race.*

KOS

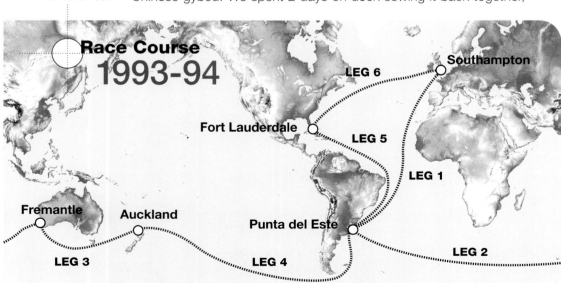

Race Course
1993-94

Southampton

LEG 6

Fort Lauderdale

LEG 5

LEG 1

Fremantle   Auckland

Punta del Este

LEG 2

LEG 3   LEG 4

even during a violent snowstorm. We also experienced the horror of a mayday from the Italian entry, *Brooksfield*. They had filled up with water near the Kerguelen Islands when their rudder ripped out. There was a numb silence on board our boat for many days as we waited for the report saying that the crew was safe. On this leg Lawrie Smith sailed the Whitbread 60 *Intrum Justitia* to a new 24-hour record—425 nautical miles—and was also first into Fremantle.

Sailing into Fremantle was most memorable for me. I'd survived my first venture into the Southern Ocean and I was feeling very proud. With the Heineken deal in place we became 'stars'—shuffled between PR events and corporate dinners by the sponsor. Heineken also promised us as much beer as we could drink! Who needed money!

The 10-day leg from Fremantle to Auckland saw *Tokio* and *New Zealand Endeavour* locked in a nail-biting finish, and the tension between the Whitbread 60 and maxi skippers flared. The passionate New Zealand media and the public made no secret of their love-hate relationship with *Tokio's*

Dickson, and their love relationship with *New Zealand Endeavour's* Dalton. The race was rarely out of the headlines.

We left Auckland in February '94 destined for another taste of the Southern Ocean. By then we had a good team on board and we were sailing the boat well. The memories of seeing my first-ever iceberg and sailing around the legendary Cape Horn are indelible. It was a rough approach to the Horn, with northwest–northeast gales blowing, just like you read about in books. *Tokio* went to an amazing latitude 61° South on approach to the Horn. Meanwhile, we discovered that the bottom half of our rudder had broken off. We sailed the rest of the leg into Punta Del Este at 80 percent of our capacity. We did not see many boats on that leg, except for huge fleets of boats fishing for squid at night off the coast of South America. The loom of their brilliant lights made them look like a floating city.

The Whitbread 60s again showed great speed on this leg: first *Yamaha* broke *Intrum's* record by 2 nautical miles, then *Intrum Justitia* soon had it back with a run of 428 nautical miles.

It was rough going off the Brazilian coast in strong headwinds and as a result our bow started to delaminate. We used bunks to reinforce the panels. *Dolphin & Youth* had a similar problem and *Tokio* lost their mast, giving *Yamaha* the chance to take the lead. *Yamaha* made a winning move in the Doldrums and sailed into Fort Lauderdale first.

Lauderdale was where I had joined our yacht, so I was thrilled to have completed a circumnavigation. However I was far from prepared for the controversy that greeted me soon after arriving. It began when our deposed skipper, Nance Frank, found remnants of a Satcom message I had sent during the leg to *Yamaha's* skipper, New Zealander Ross Field.

Lawrie Smith argued that I'd provided *Yamaha* with outside assistance. He said that I had helped *Yamaha* via general chat about the conditions during that leg. Being thrust onto the world stage and labeled a cheat on the front pages of the *The Times* in London was a shock, especially when it was really all quite innocent. After several nerve-wrecking days we were both cleared of cheating charges, but it was an eye opener for me on the politics played at this level of racing.

I remember the last leg for the thick fog. It was dangerous sailing over the Grand Banks, where there were many fishing boats on the radar but invisible in real life: both *Yamaha* and *Dolphin & Youth* had near collisions with them. This leg was the worst emotional roller coaster of the race: it might have been an adventure, but I was ready for it to be over.

With only 1,000 miles to the finish we sailed our best 6 hours in the race, clocking 102 nautical miles, but our elation quickly turned to despair when the rudder sheared off. After strengthening the transom with fibreglass and fitting the jury rudder, we set off for England at a painful 3–5 knots. With relief we sailed up the Solent and over the line a week later—joy and sadness wrapped in one.

Skipper Dawn Riley and navigator Adrienne Cahalan of the Whitbread 60 Heineken *study a navigation chart.*

1993–94 Results

Position	Yacht	Nationality	Skipper	Elapsed Time [days / hours]
Maxi Class				
1	New Zealand Endeavor	New Zealand	Grant Dalton	120d 5h
2	Merit Cup	Switzerland	Pierre Fehlman	121d 2h
3	La Poste	France	Eric Tabarly	123d 22h
4	Uruguay National	Uruguay	Gustavo Vanzini	144d 20h
Whitbread 60 Class				
1	Yamaha	Japan	Ross Field	120d 14h
2	Intrum Justitia	Europe	Lawrie Smith	121d 5h
3	Galicia '93 Pescanova	Spain	Javier Gandara	122d 6h
4	Winston	USA	Brad Butterworth	122d 9h
5	Tokio	Japan	Chris Dickson	128d 16h
6	Brooksfield	Italy	Guido Maisto	130d 4h
7	Hetman Sahaidachny	Ukraine	Eugene Platon	135d 23h
8	Dolphin & Youth	United Kingdom	Matt Humphries	137d 21h
9	Heineken	USA	Dawn Riley	138d 16h
10	Odessa	Ukraine	Anatoly Verba	158d 4h

Ebullient Swedish sailing legend **Magnus Olsson** sailed in five round-the-world contests, but many of his best memories come from the 1997–98 race and the winning *EF Language* campaign skippered by American champion, Paul Cayard. As well as being a crewmember aboard the yacht that crushed the opposition, Olsson was a coordinator of the entire campaign. The 2005–06 Volvo Ocean Race was the first where he stayed ashore and took on the sole role of team manager.

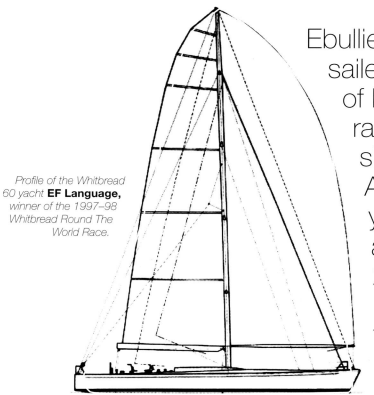

Profile of the Whitbread 60 yacht **EF Language,** *winner of the 1997–98 Whitbread Round The World Race.*

Race Seven 1997–98

The *EF Language* campaign was hugely successful on the water, but it was what happened behind the scenes, before the race even started, that was very interesting. What few outsiders know is that we sold our original skipper, Lawrie Smith, to the *Silk Cut* campaign for a lot of money.

I think this was the first time anyone has ever sold a sailor as we did—just like you sell a football player—all because we held his contract, and *Silk Cut* wanted him.

When Lawrie learned of the *Silk Cut* opportunity he came to us and said 'the *Silk Cut* deal is probably better for me because it's an English campaign, and I'm English'. Even so, he wouldn't have minded staying with us. We started negotiations with *Silk Cut* and before long they decided they had to buy him. So we let him go, and in return got this big pile of money. It was fantastic because it meant we could run an even better campaign.

Far right: Magnus Olsson, the project manager of Team EF pops his head out of EF Language.

> We already knew we had a new skipper before the *Silk Cut* deal was done. That pleased us a lot, and I'm sure it pleased the girls as well because Paul's also a very handsome guy.

It was because we didn't announce that we'd sold Lawrie to *Silk Cut* that everyone assumed he'd just quit our campaign and gone to theirs. There were plenty of people saying 'what are those EF guys doing? Have they lost their minds? How could they let Lawrie Smith go?' Certainly all the girls sailing on our second boat, *EF Education*, thought we were completely stupid—but that was because Lawrie was always the girls' favourite.

What no one outside our management team knew, was that while the negotiations were going on with *Silk Cut*, we'd called Paul Cayard and talked to him about coming in as our replacement skipper, and he had agreed. So we already knew we had a new skipper before the *Silk Cut* deal was done. That pleased us a lot, and I'm sure it pleased the girls as well because Paul's also a very handsome guy.

We'd spoken to some other possible skippers as well as Paul. Our thinking was influenced by what Chris Dickson did as a newcomer to the race 4 years earlier. We came to the conclusion that an around-the-buoys sailor, who also liked ocean racing, was what was needed. Paul had that background. Paul said two very good things to us: he hated to lose—and we wanted to hear that—and then he said to me 'Magnus, remember one thing: I never get beaten by Lawrie Smith.' That really made us laugh. I loved hearing that. We also talked about him not having done a round-the-world race, and he even had the perfect answer for that, 'If you like sailing as much as I do, then this must be the perfect thing to do, because you sail 24 hours a day!'

When Lawrie departed he took most of the team with him, so we hardly had a campaign left. But then Paul started bringing in his own people, like Kimo Worthington, Steve Erickson, Curtis Blewitt, and Rodney Ardern—so things began to look pretty good for us again. We'd gone from being a very strong English campaign to a very strong American campaign: we were on a roll, building two nice boats and putting together two good teams.

Paul is a great driving force and we got stronger and stronger during our preparation for the race. I give Paul a lot of the credit for driving the

campaign the way he did, even though he was only there 25 percent of the time before the start.

My thinking, when the race started, was that we had to have a good first leg, otherwise our campaign could tip the wrong way. As it turned out we sailed into beautiful Cape Town in November 1997 as really decisive winners. It was fantastic, and that gave us the strength we needed for the whole campaign. We still knew we were going to have ups and downs, but we also knew that we were going to be tough.

The second leg, to Fremantle, was a disaster for us. We didn't sail the boat well, Paul was very stressed in the Southern Ocean and we pushed the boat way too hard, and had a lot of problems and breakages. In Fremantle, the atmosphere was not good. It was a reality check, though,

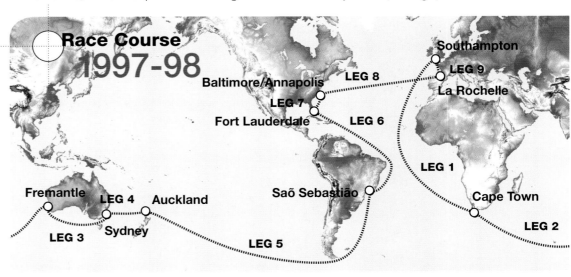

Race Course 1997-98

Southampton
LEG 9
La Rochelle
LEG 8
Baltimore/Annapolis
LEG 7
Fort Lauderdale
LEG 6
LEG 1
São Sebastião
Cape Town
LEG 2
Fremantle LEG 4 Auckland
LEG 3 Sydney
LEG 5

Our winning margin into São Sebastião was monstrous—around 3 days. Paul really enjoyed that and we all began thinking 'we can win this race,' and we did.

and I think that was good. Even so, Paul was always growling 'we have to get much better.'

We went into the next leg, to Sydney, feeling strong. We got it right and won, so we were back on our high platform. By the end of the fourth leg into Auckland we had started to sail the boat very well, because Paul backed off from his 'do it my way' attitude, to acting much more as a coach. He motivated us in a good way and let us take the responsibility we wanted to sail the boat the way we thought it should be sailed. The atmosphere on board improved and we started to joke that Paul was actually human sometimes. We sailed our boat extremely well on the next leg to Brazil: our winning margin into São Sebastiaõ was monstrous—around 3 days. Paul really enjoyed that and we all began thinking 'we can win this race,' and we did.

When I look back on the memories of the entire race there was one silly, yet funny, situation that probably proved to be a turning point for us. Paul got really upset one day when he woke up and saw three pairs of sunglasses hanging on a string on a leeward bunk. For him everything, absolutely everything, had to be on the windward side, and we'd missed moving those sunglasses. He started growling at everyone, saying 'you have to be more professional.' I said, 'take it easy Paul. There's no need to

Swedish Match leads the chasing group at the start of the third leg, off Fremantle.

be like that,' but he still was going growl, growl, growl about being more professional. So we thought 'stuff him. There's only one thing to do,' and the next time he woke up in his bunk he looked down to leeward and saw every pair of sunglasses on the boat hanging there on the string. All we heard was a shout of 'Aaaagh!' as though he was having a nightmare. But then he realised what was going on and he got the message about his behaviour. He saw the humorous side of things. That was a good way to deal with Paul sometimes. You had to confront him. He had a killer instinct but he also had to be human.

1997–98 Results

Position	Yacht	Nationality	Skipper(s)	Points
1	EF Language	Sweden	Paul Cayard	836
2	Merit Cup	Monaco	Grant Dalton	698
3	Swedish Match	Sweden	Gunnar Krantz	689
4	Innovation Kvaerner	Norway	Knut Frostad	633
5	Silk Cut	United Kingdom	Lawrie Smith	630
6	Chessie Racing	United States	George Collins	613
7	Toshiba	United States	Dennis Conner, Paul Standbridge	528
8	BrunelSunergy	Netherlands	Hans Bouscholte, Roy Heiner	415
9	EF Education	Sweden	Christine Guillou	275

1 BOAT DID NOT FINISH THE RACE: *America's Challenge*, United States.

STEVE MUNDAY

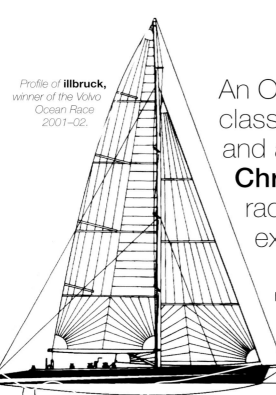

An Olympian, triple world champion in the 505 and 49er dinghy classes, two-time Australian 18-foot Skiff Grand Prix Champion, and a two-time Volvo Ocean Race competitor, little wonder that **Chris Nicholson** is one of the world's most valued offshore racing sailors. Incredibly though, his first-ever ocean racing experience was only in the 2001–02 Volvo Ocean Race.

I became a professional sailor because I was all but pushed into it by my boss when I was working as an electrical engineer in the coalmines north of Sydney. He told me that I was taking too much time off to go sailing, so I had two choices: concentrate on my work or join the unemployed. I chose sailing.

After the Sydney Olympics in 2000 I decided that I wanted to get out of dinghy racing and try something different, and the Volvo Ocean Race was my immediate choice. I knew Paul Cayard was involved with the *Amer Sports One* programme so I contacted him through a friend. The email finished up on Grant Dalton's desk—he was the skipper—and the message I got back was 'come over to France and try out.'

Now this is where I have to make a confession. On my resume I didn't say that I got chronically seasick, and because the application didn't ask specifically about offshore racing experience, I simply said 'raced off Australia's east coast,' which, in fact, meant that I'd done one Sydney-to-Southport race and spent a total of 2 nights at sea. Needless to say, for the 3 months I was in France, working on the boat before it was launched, I was forever nervous about being found out. Making things worse was that I'd realised you steered the boat via instruments—by numbers—and I'd never done that before! My great fear was that I was wasting my time being there, but more so theirs. But I was there and had to give it a shot.

Race Eight 2001–02

Once the yacht was launched I found the day training on the Mediterranean easy—there's no need to spend any time below deck and generally it's not rough. But the moment we set out on a 9-day passage, I felt like my life was going to end: I was incredibly seasick, so sick that I had no option but to go to 'Dalts,' who had been aboard *Amer Sports Two* for the trip, and say, 'I got really crook on the trip and I might not be able to do things properly.' But I didn't want to quit, so I offered to stay on deck for an extra watch so I wouldn't have to go below. In typical Dalts fashion he said, 'You've done a great job. Just hang in there.' He then offered to take my turn doing the dishes so I wouldn't have to go below. That's the sort of man he is.

The start of the race was a baptism by fire for me. I was told I was a helmsman, but I don't think it was until 3 months after the start that I felt my skills were anything like that of the others. There I was trying to understand apparent wind angle, true wind angle, boat heel, boat speed. I realised one night that I was trying to process seven different things at one time, and that I probably wasn't smart enough to do it. It was an awful feeling. Now it's just second nature.

With this being my first offshore campaign, I couldn't believe that the boats could smash their way upwind as they did and not break in half. I remember saying to Dalts 'when do we back off? I'm not worried about it

but it just seems odd to me; it seems like we're going to smash this boat to bits.' And he'd just say, 'Oh well, it feels that way but the guy beside us won't back off, so if he won't back off then we won't back off.' Those boats were so tough that you would just shake your head in disbelief, not able to understand how they could withstand such punishment and just keep crashing over wave after wave.

It was leg four in this race that I really remember. It was full on: plenty of breeze, icebergs, and big seas. Dalts even admitted that it was the most intense, stressful sailing he'd ever done. I think that, at one stage, there were five off-watches where I didn't get any sleep. At one point it was so bad that Bouwe (Bekking), Paul (Cayard), and I went out of the watch system, because Dalts decided that we were the only three drivers capable of keeping the thing upright. We rotated non-stop as drivers, just to get through the worst of the weather. At the time I thought we had only done this for 2 days, but it turned out that we'd done it for near 5. There was no recollection of time for us. I don't think I've ever been so physically stressed as I was then, and I was struggling to come to terms with enjoying the race. But by the time we got to Rio the pain had gone and I knew I wanted to do the Southern Ocean again, even though other guys were saying 'never again.'

My worst day on the boat during the entire race had nothing to do with the sailing. I was down the back washing the dishes in a bucket on deck, partly because, if I went below and used the galley, I'd be seasick. Once I finished, I tipped the dirty water that was in the bucket over the side, and as I did I thought I saw just a glint of silver reflect in the sun. All I could think was 'Oh No.' I knew that I'd had all our spoons in the bucket, so I put my hand in there and sure enough; there was nothing to be found. Now I'm far from a dishonest person, but I must admit that I panicked. I asked myself 'should I just pretend it never happened? Then I thought 'No. They'll all know it was me because I was the last person that washed up.' So I casually walked back towards the cabin and said to Dalts in passing 'Oh well, I've just had the biggest f'-up in the world. I've turfed all the spoons over the side.' As if he was unconcerned, Dalts just said 'well, you better get your arse downstairs and sort something out.' As I went below, wondering what on earth I could do to create some spoons, I looked to my left and there, in

Race Course
2001–02

LEG 8 Göteborg
Southampton LEG 9
Baltimore/ Kiel
Annapolis LEG 7
La Rochelle
LEG 6
Miami
LEG 5
LEG 1
Sydney Rio de Janeiro
Auckland Cape Town
LEG 3 LEG 2
LEG 4

CARLO BORLENGHI / SEA&SEE

saying something like 'don't think I'm being nice to you.'

For me Grant Dalton is a legend, a tremendous leader who will do anything on board, any job at any time, just to keep things happening. He's got the right manner to bring the right people together and never lets ego get in the way of getting a job done. Most people only see the tough exterior, but beneath it I've always found he was pretty soft . . . and that's something I know he won't like to hear.

Our problem in the 2001–02 race was that we were a late campaign, so we never saw the best from the boat. But it was a great credit to Dalts and Bouwe that we didn't break anything. That was a big achievement.

I knew when the race was over that I would have to go again, and that decision was made even easier with the news of the new class, the Volvo Open 70. I don't think I would have done it again if they'd stuck with the Volvo Ocean 60: the challenge wouldn't have been there, but to do it in a new design and a cool boat, oh for sure. And as for seasickness, well I still get the occasional dusty moment, but thanks to some special motion sickness medication and hypnosis I've just about got it beaten.

front of me, were all the brand new, $1,000-a-pop Ferragamo sunglasses from one of our sponsors. The lenses were the perfect shape, so I grabbed a small screwdriver and ripped apart four pairs of the sunglasses. There, instantly, were our spoons. Dalts asked if I'd fixed the problem, and I said, 'you'll see.' Later I served him his meal with his sunglasses, minus the lenses, hanging out of the bowl. He liked it, even though each spoon cost $500. Somehow though, I don't think it was quite the image that Mr. Ferragamo wanted for his sunglasses.

Dalts was the watch captain on my watch, and it seemed that every time the heinous weather arrived, he'd get me to drive, and just leave me there. I felt that the guy had blind faith in me just because I never capsized the thing: but he and the rest of the crew never knew how often I came close to losing control, especially when it was blowing more than 40 knots. I was right on the edge of my skills, but Dalts always showed confidence in me. I remember that whenever we took a massive nosedive and water came rushing down the deck, and I was struggling to hang onto the wheel, I'd feel a hand or a foot planted firmly in the middle of my back just to hold me there. It was Dalts, sitting there smiling, helping me stay in place and

The fleet of Volvo Ocean 60s at the start of leg five.

2001–02 Results

Position	Yacht	Nationality	Skipper	Points
1	illbruck	United States	John Kostecki	61
2	Assa Abloy	United Kingdom	Neal McDonald	55
3	Amer Sports One	New Zealand	Grant Dalton	44
4	Tyco	New Zealand	Kevin Shoebridge	42
5	News Corp	United Kingdom	Jez Fanstone	41
6	djuice	Norway	Knut Frostad	33
7	SEB	Sweden	Gunnar Krantz	32
8	Amer Sports Too	United Kingdom/ United States	Lisa McDonald	16

The Black Pearl *on its way
into the Southern Ocean after
the start of leg four.*

Th

In every sense, the Volvo Ocean Race 2005–06 was the mediator in a test of character. It could change your perspective on everything, keep you grounded, and broaden your horizons. It was a litmus test of the human spirit.

The fact that we ventured to the edge of the unknown with this edition of the race certainly influenced that test. For us there was no stepping back. We had to face new challenges if we were to continue to lay claim to being at the absolute pinnacle of extreme sport: We could not be afraid to be innovators.

We took the world of international offshore sailing into a new realm with the introduction of the Volvo Open 70, a revolutionary concept that delivered everything that we had hoped for.

eFinishLine

Top: Movistar *heads out of Port Phillip Bay on the way to Mebourne.*
Right: Brasil 1 *during the in-port race in Portsmouth.*

On the first leg to Cape Town, *ABN AMRO ONE* became the world's fastest single-hulled sailboat on a 24-hour run, and subsequently *ABN AMRO TWO* set an amazing new mark—563 nautical miles in a day. Like anything that is revolutionary, the new design wasn't without its problems in the early stages, but by the time the circumnavigation was complete it had moved from revolutionary to evolutionary and was being acclaimed worldwide.

Another bold step was an innovative new course and a more challenging racing format, including the introduction of in-port races. For the first time, we turned the competition into a spectator sport for hundreds of thousands of people.

The race also reminded us of what had been known for the preceding 33 years of its history—that crews are never far from great danger as they cross the world's wildest and most remote stretches of ocean. That reminder came so abruptly and sadly with the loss of Hans Horrevoets from *ABN AMRO TWO* on the leg from New York to Portsmouth. This tragedy challenged every fibre of the race, and it was through outstanding human endeavour and great spirit on the part of the yacht's crew and our race management team that the entire search and rescue operation was conducted in such a professional manner. Incredibly, just hours later, while our hearts shared the grief being endured by Hans' partner, Petra, and his family, the same people

were tested again when the *ABN AMRO TWO* team rose to the call and rescued the crew of *movistar* after it was abandoned.

We go into this race knowing that sailing 32,000 nautical miles around the globe will never be easy, simple, or just plain sailing, and, as a consequence, the impact of the event over the 8 months of competition has left an indelible mark on everyone associated with it—the sailors, race management, shore teams, sponsors, and the traveling media. All faced more challenges over the period than they could normally expect in a decade, and in dealing with those challenges, good and bad, everyone has come away richer for the experience.

For some of us there were life-changing experiences that came because of the race but beyond the sailing, like our visit to the shantytowns in Cape Town where millions live a life that must be seen to be understood. It's a microcosm of refugees from Zimbabwe, Botswana, and Ethiopia, some of whom had walked in bare feet for hundreds, and sometimes thousands of miles in search of a better place to live. We saw poverty and malnourishment firsthand and it shocked us. This raw experience brought more powerful meaning and determination to our efforts to utilise the unique opportunities we are presented with through the global nature of the Volvo Ocean Race and make it far more than a sporting contest.

Sailing 32,000 nautical miles around the globe will never be easy, simple, or just plain sailing, and, as a consequence, the impact of the event over the 8 months of competition has left an indelible mark on everyone associated with it.

We introduced this element before the start by embracing the 'Save the Albatross' campaign. We wanted the Volvo Ocean Race to generate greater global awareness of the threat that long-line fishing is bringing to the existence of these magnificent birds of the Southern Ocean.

However, it was during the pitstop in New York that the Volvo Ocean Race made its greatest mark beyond sailing. It was the Gala Dinner for the World Childhood Foundation, organised jointly by Volvo in America and our own events team. H.M. King Carl XVI Gustaf and H.M. Queen Silvia of Sweden were present, along with ambassadors, senators and senior politicians, senior executives from Volvo and our yacht sponsors, plus senior executives from a broad cross section of American business. It was an engaging, meaningful, and immensely successful night, raising $US 670,000 for the World Childhood Foundation: possibly the largest amount ever. Founded by Queen Silvia 'to give children at risk a chance for a secure and happy childhood,' the Foundation currently supports 75 projects in 15 countries.

Our media achievements were at record levels this time—an accumulated international television audience of around 2 billion, a 1 billion+ radio audience, and unprecedented coverage in print. Proud as we are of these success stories it cannot be forgotten that without the sailors, their sponsors, and Volvo there would be no Volvo Ocean Race, so we are indebted to them in every sense.

There is no doubt that this latest race was very much a turning point, a defining moment, in the great history of this contest. And because of this the Volvo Ocean Race 2008-09 promises a powerful and exciting expansion of what a sporting challenge is, a challenge that, as we saw this time, takes life to the outer limits of 'extreme.' We will again be racing the Volvo Open 70s, and this time the course is destined to take us to even more exciting frontiers and the largest audience ever.

Glenn Bourke
CEO, Volvo Ocean Race

Clockwise from left: The sun breaks through the waves breaking across ABN AMRO TWO during leg six.

Richard Mason trims the jib on Ericsson with a view of a fiery sky and England ahead.

All awash on deck on ABN AMRO ONE during leg three.

Final Results Table

Position	Yacht	Sanxenxo In-Port Race	Scoring Gate One	Leg One	Cape Town In-Port Race	Scoring Gate Two	Scoring Gate Three	Leg Two	Melbourne In-Port Race	Leg Three	Scoring Gate Four	Leg Four	Rio In-Port Race
1	ABN AMRO ONE	1	3.5	7	3.5	3.5	3.5	7	3.5	6	3.5	7	3.5
2	The Black Pearl	2.5	0	1	1.5	2.5	2	4	3	5	3	6	1
3	Brasil 1	3	2.5	5	2	1	0	1	1.5	4	2.5	4	2
4	ABN AMRO TWO	1.5	2	6	2.5	3	3	6	1	3	2	5	1.5
5	Ericsson	3.5	3	4	1	0	0	1	2	2	1.5	3	2.5
6	movistar	2	0	1	3	2	2.5	5	2.5	7	1	2	3
7	Brunel	0	1.5	3	0.5	1.5	1.5	3	0.5				

Leg Trophies

	First	Second	Third
Leg 1	ABN AMRO ONE	ABN AMRO TWO	Brasil 1
Leg 2	ABN AMRO ONE	ABN AMRO TWO	movistar
Leg 3	movistar	ABN AMRO ONE	The Black Pearl
Leg 4	ABN AMRO ONE	The Black Pearl	ABN AMRO TWO
Leg 5	ABN AMRO ONE	movistar	The Black Pearl
Leg 6	ABN AMRO ONE	The Black Pearl	Brasil 1
Leg 7	ABN AMRO ONE	Ericsson	The Black Pearl
Leg 8	Brasil 1	ABN AMRO ONE	Ericsson
Leg 9	The Black Pearl	ABN AMRO TWO	Brasil 1

Overall Winner of the Volvo Ocean Race: ABN AMRO ONE

In-Port Trophies

	First	Second	Third
Sanxenxo	Ericsson	Brasil 1	The Black Pearl
Cape Town	ABN AMRO ONE	movistar	ABN AMRO TWO
Melbourne	ABN AMRO ONE	The Black Pearl	movistar
Rio de Janeiro	ABN AMRO ONE	movistar	Ericsson
Baltimore	movistar	Brasil 1	The Black Pearl
Portsmouth	ABN AMRO ONE	The Black Pearl	Brasil 1
Rotterdam	ABN AMRO ONE	Brasil 1	The Black Pearl

In-Port Race Series Winner: ABN AMRO ONE

This page, from top left:
Mike Sanderson of ABN AMRO ONE.
Torben Grael of Brasil 1.
The crew of The Black Pearl.

Trophies & Awa

Scoring Gate Five	Leg Five	Baltimore In-Port Race	Leg Six	Scoring Gate Six	Leg Seven	Leg Seven Redress*	Portsmouth In-Port Race	Leg Eight	Rotterdam In-Port Race	Leg Nine	Overall Points
3	7	1	7	3.5	7		3.5	6	3.5	2	96.0
2.5	5	2.5	6	2.5	5	1.5	3	4	2.5	7	73.0
1.5	4	3	5	2	4	1.5	2.5	7	3	5	67.0
1	2	1.5	1	1	2	1.5	2	3	1	6	58.5
2	3	2	4	3	6		1.5	5	2	3	55.0
3.5	6	3.5	3		1						48.0
		0.5	2	1.5	3		1	2	1.5	4	15.5**

*for turning back to assist other boats   **Brunel re-entered the event after extensive modifications and in so doing her previous points were not counted.

Other Trophies

GANT TIME PRIZE FOR THE BEST 24-HOUR RUN
ABN AMRO ONE, leg one, for 546 nautical miles in 24 hours, an average speed of 22.7 knots.

GANT TIME PRIZE FOR THE BEST 24-HOUR RUN
ABN AMRO TWO, leg two, for 563 nautical miles in 24 hours, setting a new world record.

ROARING FORTIES SAVE THE ALBATROSS TROPHY: Mike Sanderson, **ABN AMRO ONE,** for the highest aggregate points, from Cape Town to Rio de Janeiro.

Media Award

Leg 1	ABN AMRO TWO
Leg 2	Brasil 1
Leg 3	Not awarded
Leg 4	Ericsson
Leg 5	J Sobrino / M Bertrand, movistar PR team
Leg 6	Not awarded
Leg 7	movistar
Leg 8	C Green, ABN AMRO PR team
Leg 9	Not awarded

OVERALL WINNER: ABN AMRO TWO

Musto Seamanship Award

Leg 1	Richard Mason, Ericsson
Leg 2	Andrea Fonseca, Brasil 1
Leg 4	Chris Nicholson, movistar
Leg 5	Andy Meiklejohn, Brasil 1
Leg 7	Sebastien Josse & Crew of ABN AMRO TWO

OVERALL WINNER: ABN AMRO TWO

Wallenius Wilhelmsen Logistics Ocean Watch Environmental Prize

Leg 1	ABN AMRO ONE
Leg 2	The Black Pearl
Leg 3	Not awarded
Leg 4	Brasil 1
Leg 5	ABN AMRO ONE
Leg 6	Not awarded
Leg 7	Will Oxley, Brunel
Leg 8	Not awarded
Leg 9	Not awarded

OVERALL WINNER: BRASIL 1

VOLVO OCEAN RACE **LEG 8: MEDIA AWARD**
Pay **Camilla Green, Team ABN AMRO**
US$ 1,000.00
One Thousand US Dollars

This page, from left: Camilla Green receives the Media Award.

The crew of ABN AMRO TWO.

Will Oxley receives the Ocean Watch Environmental Prize.

CrewLists

ABN AMRO ONE
Mike Sanderson (NZ) Skipper
Stan Honey (USA) *Navigator*
Mark Christensen (NZ) *legs 1, 3, 4, 5, 6, 7, 8, 9*
Jan Dekker (RSA)
David Endean (NZ)
Sidney Gavignet (FRA)
Robert Greenhalgh (UK)
Brad Jackson (NZ)
Tony Mutter (NZ)
Justin Slattery (IRE)
Brian Thompson (UK) *leg 2*

ABN AMRO TWO

ABN AMRO ONE

ABN AMRO TWO

ABN AMRO TWO
Sebastien Josse (FRA) Skipper
Simon Fisher (UK) *Navigator*
Scott Beavis (NZ)
Nick Bice (AUS) *legs 1, 2, 3, 4, 6, 7, 8, 9*
Lucas Brun (BRA) *legs 4, 5, 6, 7, 8, 9*
Hans Horrevoets (NED)
Yves Leblevec (FRA) *leg 5*
Andrew Lewis (USA)
Luke Molloy (AUS)
George Peet (USA)
Gerd jan Poortman (NED) *legs 1, 2, 3, 8, 9*
Simeon Tienpont (NED)

Brasil 1

BRASIL 1
Torben Grael (BRA) Skipper
Marcel Van Triest (NED) *Navigator
    legs 2, 3, 4, 5, 6, 7, 8, 9*
Adrienne Cahalan (AUS) *Navigator leg 1*
Roberto Bermudez (ESP) *legs 1, 2, 3, 4, 5*
Horacio Carabelli (BRA) *legs 1, 3, 4, 5*
Marcelo Ferreira (BRA) *legs 1, 2, 5*
André Fonseca (BRA)
Knut Frostad (NOR) *legs 2, 3, 4*
Andrew Meiklejohn (NZ)
Henrique Pellicano (BRA) *legs 1, 2, 3, 4, 5*
João Signorini (BRA) *legs 1, 2, 3, 4, 5*
Stuart Wilson (NZ)

Brasil 1

BRUNEL
Grant Wharington (AUS) Skipper legs 1, 2, 6
**Matthew Humphries (UK) Skipper/Navigator
    legs 2, 6, 7, 8, 9**
Campbell Field (NZ) Navigator *leg 1*
William Oxley (AUS) Navigator *legs 6, 7, 8, 9*
Philip Airey (NZ) *legs 6, 7, 8, 9*
Mark Bartlett (UK) *legs 1, 7, 8, 9*
Fraser Brown (NZ) *leg 1*
Gareth Cooke (NZ) *legs 2, 6, 7, 8, 9*
Mark Fullerton (AUS) *leg 2*
Philip Harmer (AUS) *legs 6, 7, 8, 9*
Adam Hawkins (AUS) *legs 1, 2*
Ben Jones (AUS) *leg 2*
Eduard van Lierde (NED) *legs 6, 7, 8, 9*
Jeff Scott (NZ) *legs 1, 2, 6, 7, 8, 9*
Graeme Taylor (AUS) *legs 1, 6, 7, 8*
Ian Walker (AUS) *legs 1, 2*
Mitchell White (AUS) *legs 6, 7, 8, 9*

Brunel

Ericsson

ERICSSON
Neal McDonald (UK) Skipper
John Kostecki (USA) Skipper *leg 5*
Steven Hayles (UK) Navigator *legs 1, 2, 3, 4, 5*
Mark Rudiger (USA) Navigator *legs 6, 7*
Andrew Cape (AUS) Navigator *legs 8, 9*
Guillermo Altadill (ESP) *legs 1, 2, 3, 4, 5*
Richard Bouzaid (NZ) *legs 6, 7, 8*
Thomas Braidwood (AUS) *legs 1, 2, 3, 4*
Jason Carrington (UK) *legs 1, 2, 3, 4*
Damian Foxall (IRE) *legs 2, 3, 4, 5, 6, 7, 8, 9*
Ross Halcrow (NZ) *leg 5*
Tony Kolb (GER) *leg 1*
Richard Mason (NZ)
Tom McWilliam (IRE) *leg 9*
Timothy Powell (UK)
Ken Read (USA) *legs 6, 7, 8, 9*
David Rolfe (NZ)
Ian Walker (AUS) *legs 6, 7, 8, 9*
Magnus Woxen (SWE)

Ericsson

movistar

MOVISTAR
Bouwe Bekking (NED) Skipper
Andrew Cape (AUS) *Navigator*
Stu Bannatyne (NZ)
Peter Doriean (AUS)
Noel Drennan (IRE) *legs 1, 2, 3, 4, 7*
Fernando Echavarri (ESP) *legs 5, 6, 7*
Xabier Fernández (ESP) *legs 1, 2, 3, 4*
Mike Howard (USA) *leg 5*
Mike Joubert (RSA)
Chris Nicholson (AUS)
Pepe Ribes (ESP)
Jonathan Swain (USA)

movistar

The Black Pearl

The Black Pearl

THE BLACK PEARL
Paul Cayard (USA) Skipper
Jules Salter (UK) *Navigator*
Rodney Ardern (NZ)
Curtis Blewett (CAN) *legs 1, 2, 3*
Ian Budgen (UK) *legs 5, 6, 7, 8, 9*
Justin Clougher (AUS)
Dirk de Ridder (NED)
Justin Ferris (NZ) *legs 1, 2, 3*
Jerry Kirby (USA) *legs 5, 6, 7, 8, 9*
Fredrik Loof (SWE) *leg 1*
Anthony Merrington (AUS) *legs 2, 3, 4, 5, 6, 7, 8, 9*
Craig Satterthwaite (NZ) *legs 1, 2, 3*
Jeremy Smith (NZ) *leg 4*
Erle Williams (NZ)

Glossary

Aft: Towards the rear of the yacht.

Apparent Wind: The perceived wind direction of a moving yacht. When the yacht goes faster the perceived wind direction moves forward, just as the wind always seems to hit a car only from head-on as it drives at high speeds.

Abandon Ship: To leave a fatally distressed vessel.

Asymmetric: Spinnaker—a downwind sail flown from the bow of the boat.

Backstay: A mast support that runs from the top of the mast to the stern of the yacht; it may be adjustable in order to bend the mast backward or to increase tension on the forestay.

Bare Headed: A yacht without a headsail hoisted. Bare-headed change is changing headsails where one sail is completely lowered and removed before another is hoised.

Beam: A boat's greatest width.

Beating: Sailing (or pointing) at an angle into the wind or upwind. Since sailboats cannot sail directly into the wind, "beating" is the closest course to the wind they can sail.

Berth: a) The place where you put the boat on a dock; b) bunk or sleeping quarters

Bilge: The lowest part of a boat's hull.

Block: A deck or track-mounted pulley device through which ropes such as jib and genoa sheets are strung.

Boom: Spar to which a sail's lower edge or "foot" is attached. The boom is attached to the mast at the gooseneck.

Bosun's Chair: A seat, usually made of canvas, used to hoist a person up the mast.

Bow: The front of the boat.

Bowman: Crewmember in charge of sail changes and keeping a lookout on the bow at the start.

Bowsprit: A projecting spar extending from the bow of the boat. Volvo Open 70s have a 1.82-metre-long carbon fibre bowsprit on which to fly their A-sails.

Bulb: The lead-torpedo shape on the bottom of the keel.

Bulkhead: A partition to strengthen the frame of a yacht.

Buoy: A marker used for navigation, mooring, or racing around.

Canard: A fixed daggerboard.

Canting Keel: A keel hinged at the bottom of the hull and moved from side to side by massive hydraulic rams. This enables the crew to swing the ballast bulb to the windward side of the boat to counteract the forces trying to heel over the boat.

Capsize: Turning upside down.

Chainplates: The metal or composite attachments for shrouds and stays. Part of the hull, connecting the hull with the rig.

Chute: Spinnaker.

Checkstay: A small additional sub-set of the running backstays often attached just below the spreaders on a multi-spreader rig to prevent the mast from pumping backward and forwards in a seaway and overbending.

Chinese Gybe: An accidental gybe where the boom is trapped by a line and prevented from swinging fully across the boat. Usually the boat rounds up violently and is knocked on its side.

Clew: The lower corner of a mainsail, jib or genoa and either lower corner of a spinnaker attached to the sheet.

Cockpit: A recessed area in the deck in which the crew works.

Code 0: Tight luff, upwind spinnaker developed by *EF Language* during the 1997-98 Whitbread race, also called "the Whomper."

Compass: An instrument that uses the earth's magnetic field to point to the direction of the magnetic North Pole; used by navigators to determine the direction a yacht is heading and to set a course.

Course: The direction a yacht is sailing.

Crew: The team of sailors that sail the yacht.

Daggerboard: One or two fitted forward of the mast to supply lateral resistance when the canting keel is swung out to the side to keep the boat upright.

Dead Downwind: Sailing with the wind.

Deck: Horizontal surface of a yacht.

Delaminating: Failure of the bond between either of the hull's outer and inner skins, and the "sandwich" spacing material in between—allowing either of the two outer layers to become unstuck from the core.

Desalinator: A machine that takes salt water and forces it at extremely high pressure through a special membrane, which traps the salt and only allows fresh water through.

Dismast: To lose, through breakage, part or all of the mast.

Doldrums: Area between weather systems of the Northern and Southern Hemispheres characterised by frustrating light winds, major shifts in wind direction, and sudden violent squalls.

Downwind: The point of sail when the wind blows from aft of the yacht's beam.

Endoscope: A device inserted through the hull just ahead of the rudder or keel to see if anything, such as weed or large fish, is wrapped around the foils.

EPIRB: Emergency Position Indicating Radio Beacon. There are two types of beacon; one is a transmitter that all commercial vessels are required to have on board. The second type is a personal EPIRB that sailors wear on themselves, either as a watch, within their clothing, or around their neck so they can be located should they be washed overboard.

Equator: Line of latitude at 0 degrees—an equal distance from both poles.

Foot: The bottom edge of a sail.

Foredeck: The area of a yacht's deck that is in front of the mast; also a crew position aboard a racing yacht.

Foresail: Any sail used between the mast and the forestay.

Forestay: A mast support that runs from the top of the mast, or near the top of the mast, to the bow.

Fractional Rig: A rig where the headstay does not go to the top of the mast.

Freeze Dried: Lightweight food, which looks like soup powder with lumps, reconstituted by mixing with boiling water.

Front: A weather front is a line representing the transition between two air masses.

Furious Fifties: Area between 50 degrees and 60 degrees latitude noted for very strong winds and huge seas.

Galley: Kitchen.

Gennaker: Cross between a genoa and a spinnaker, a foresail used for reaching.

Genoa: A large foresail that overlaps the shroud base and used for sailing upwind; also called a "genny."

GPS: Global Positioning System. Satellite navigation, which gives yachts exact latitude and longitude position. The update rate is one second.

Guy: A rope used to adjust the position of a spinnaker pole.

Gybe: Turning the yacht so that the stern of the yacht turns through the wind, thereby changing the side of the yacht on which the sails are carried (opposite of tacking); also spelled jibe.

Gooseneck: The mechanical device connecting the boom and the mast.

Grinder: The winch system operated by the pedestal system. The crewmember who is using the pedestal system.

Halyard: A line used to hoist and hold up a sail.

Harness: Life harness, a webbing harness worn about the torso, with a detachable tether, intended to prevent a crewmember falling overboard and becoming detached from the boat

Head: a) Toilet/Basin/Shower; b) the top corner of a sail that is connected to the halyard.

Header: Wind shift so the wind enters the boat more forward.

Headsail: Sail flown between the mast and the bow of the yacht.

Helm: The steering station of a yacht; the tiller or wheel by which the rudder is controlled.

Helmsman: The crewmember who steers the yacht, usually also the skipper; also called the "driver."

Hounds: The attachment points for the shrouds up the mast.

Hull: The body of a yacht.

Inmarsat-C: A digital store and forward messaging service, using satellites for transmission.

Jib: A foresail that fits in between the forestay and the mast.

Jury-rig: Emergency rigging with available gear, usually involves a broken mast.

Kevlar: Man-made, yellow/brown aramid fibre used to make sails or composites for building hulls.

Kite: Spinnaker.

Knockdown: Occurs when a yacht heels 90 degrees or more, usually as a result of heavy winds or wave action or a combination.

Knot: a) One nautical mile per hour (equals 1.15 miles/1.825 km); b) connection of lines.

Latitude: Angular distance north or south of equator; measured from 0 to 90 degrees north or south.

Layline: An imaginary line projecting at an angle corresponding to the wind direction from either side of a racecourse marker buoy that defines the optimum sailing angle for a yacht to fetch to the mark or the finish line. When a yacht reaches this point, it is said to be "on the layline." Going beyond the layline means the yacht is sailing a greater distance to reach the mark or finish line.

Leech: Trailing edge of a sail.

Leeward: Used as an adjective to mean away from the wind. A leeward yacht is one that has another yacht between it and the wind (opposite of windward).

Life Raft: An inflatable craft into which the crew of a yacht transfers if the yacht intends to sink.

Lifelines: Cables that are held in place by stanchions and go around the boat to prevent people falling overboard. A "fence" around the boat on the edge of the deck.

Lift: A wind shift so the wind enters the boat from further back. That allows either the helmsman to head up or alter course to windward, or the crew to ease sheets.

Lines: A nautical term for ropes.

Longitude: Angular distance east or west of the Greenwich Meridian, measured from 0 to 180 degrees east or west.

Luff: a) to change course towards the wind; b) the leading edge of a sail.

Mainsheet Trimmer: Controls the position and shape of the mainsail, the large triangular sail behind the mast.

Mast: The vertical spar that holds up the sails.

Mastman: The crewmember that works the lines on the mast when hoisting sails and who assists the bowman with the work on the foredeck.

Masthead Rig: A rigging scheme in which the forestay is attached near the top, of the mast. See Fractional Rig.

Match Racing: A racing format where only two yachts compete at a time, like a boxing match, as opposed to "fleet racing" where more yachts sail at once.

Nautical Mile: The unit of geographical

distance used on "salt-water" charts. One nautical mile corresponds exactly to one minute of angular distance on the meridian (adjacent left and right side of a sea chart). This facilitates navigation as it avoids a complicated conversion from angle to distance. One nautical mile equals 1,852 metres. Sixty minutes equal 1 degree.

Navigator: The crewmember who monitors the yacht's location and progress relative to the racecourse and the opposing yacht.

Off the Wind: Sailing away from the wind, also downwind, reaching, or running.

Peeling: Changing from one spinnaker to another.

Pitch-poling: Putting the bow into a wave and cartwheeling forward.

Pitman: Crewmember that controls the halyards and mast winches; assists the mastman.

Pole: Spinnaker pole.

Port: Nautical term for the left side of a yacht when facing forward.

Port Tack: Sailing with the wind blowing onto the port side and the mainsail on the starboard side.

Reaching: All angles against the wind that are not beating or dead downwind. Close Reach – Beam Reach – Broad Reach.

RIB: A rigid bottom inflatable boat.

Rig: The general term used to describe a yacht's mast and sail combination.

Rigging: The wires, lines, halyards, and other items used to attach the sails and the spars to the boat. The lines that do not have to be adjusted often are known as standing rigging. The lines that are adjusted to raise, lower, and trim the sails are known as running rigging.

Roaring Forties: Area between 40 degrees and 50 degrees latitude noted for strong winds and large seas.

Running: Dead downwind.

Sail Turtle: A soft pack in which headsails that are not in use are folded and stowed.

Screaming Sixties: Area between 60 degrees and 70 degrees latitude noted for exceptionally strong wind, huge seas, and frequent icebergs.

Sheet: A line that controls sails and adjusts their angle of attack and their trailing edge.

Shroud: Cable or rod that supports the mast sidewise. They run from the chainplates at deck level on the port and starboard side, to the hounds just below the top of the mast.

Southern Ocean: The ocean surrounding the Antarctic continent is the largest uninterrupted water on earth and creates the most dynamic weather systems, the highest waves, and the strongest winds (apart from tropical storms).

Spinnaker: Large ballooning sail that is flown in front of the yacht when the wind comes from abaft abeam. They are used when running or reaching, sailing downwind. Also called Kite or Chute.

Spinnaker Pole: A pole that is attached to the lower front of the mast to hold one corner of a spinnaker out from the yacht. On high-performance yachts, spinnaker poles are usually made of strong but lightweight carbon fibre composite material. When a spinnaker is not being flown, the pole is tethered to the deck.

Squall: The sudden, short-termed burst of wind with clouds passing. Can be accompanied by rain.

Stanchions: Vertical poles that stand on the outer edge of the deck to hold the lifelines.

Standing Rigging: The non-moving rods and lines that support the mast and sails.

Starboard: Nautical term for the right half of the yacht when facing forward.

Starboard Tack: Sailing with the wind blowing onto the starboard side, and the mainsail on the port side.

Staysail: A small sail flown between the mast and the inner forestay.

Stay: A rod or wire that supports the mast in a fore/aft position.

Tack: a) turning the bow of the yacht through the wind and changing the sides of the sails; b) the lower corner of a sail that is attached to the yacht.

Trade Wind: Northeast and southeast winds in the Atlantic blowing continually toward the equator. Named after the traditional trading ships, which sailed a course using these winds to their advantage.

Transom: The flat rear end of a boat.

Trim: To adjust the sail to make it the right shape and angle to the wind.

Trysail: A triangular loose-footed sail fitted aft of the mast, often used to replace the mainsail in heavy weather.

Upwind: Sailing against the wind at an angle a certain yacht can achieve.

Velocity Made Good (VMG): The speed of a yacht relative to the waypoint it wants to reach or towards or away from the wind.

Watches: Teams within which the crew operates, taking turns to work, sleep, and eat.

Watch Leader/Captain: The person in charge of a watch.

Watertight Hatch: Each yacht is equipped with several watertight doors, or hatches. In the event of a hull breach, the hatches can be closed to seal off compartments on the affected portion of the boat.

Winch: A device used to give a mechanical advantage when hauling on the lines.

Winch Pedestal: Upright winch drive mechanism with two handles—increases purchasing power.

Windward: Against the wind.

Photograp

THE FINISH LINE

OSKAR KIHLBORG

Originally one of Sweden's best mountaineers, **official Volvo Ocean Race photographer**, Oskar Kihlborg, changed career and began working as a sailing photographer in 1993. Kihlborg, well known for his intense images of people, was responsible for showing the world, through his captivating images, what the Volvo Ocean Race 2005–06 was all about: the happiness, the sorrow, the sweat and the tears, the high tech and mother nature. Following the conclusion of the event, Kihlborg was appointed official photographer to *Victory Challenge*, the Swedish entry in the 2007 America's Cup.

MARÍA MUIÑA

Maria has been freelancing as a sailing photographer since 2002 and first worked with the movistar Sailing Team in Spain. After working for several other racing teams and yacht clubs, Maria was hired as the official photographer to *movistar* and covered the Volvo Ocean Race for the team.

DAVID BRANIGAN

David Branigan is a marine photographer based in Dublin, Ireland. He first covered the Whitbread Race in 1989–90 before returning as the official photographer in 1993–94 and team photographer for Lawrie Smith's *Silk Cut* in 1997–98. For 2005–06, he travelled to every stopover as a freelance photographer retained by Volvo Event Management, The Mobile Channel, *movistar,* and *Brunel* amongst others.

JON NASH

Jon Nash is a top UK-based sailing photographer. He was chosen by TEAM ABN AMRO to document the entire Volvo Ocean Race two-boat campaign and traveled to each of the nine stopovers to capture the excitement. His brief was simple: to come back with amazing shots of the race. This was Jon's third Whitbread/Volvo Ocean Race as a photographer and he says it has been one of the most challenging, but most exciting and rewarding shoots to date.

hers

PAUL TODD

Paul Todd is a former professional sailor and spends much of his time travelling around the world photographing regattas such as the America's Cup, Whitbread and Volvo Ocean Races, as well as world championship and superyacht projects. Following the Volvo Ocean Race 2005–06, Paul spent the summer in Europe shooting for international yachting and lifestyle magazines and commercial clients.

RICK TOMLINSON

Rick Tomlinson had competed as a crew member in four Whitbread Round The World Races prior to being the official photographer for the first-ever Volvo Ocean Race in 2001–02. For the 2005–06 edition he worked for Ericsson Racing Team alongside his friend and colleague, Thierry Martinez. Based in Cowes Isle of Wight, UK, Rick works exclusively in yachting and his assignments take him all over the world, photographing both the great yachts, and the great yacht races.

GEORGE JOHNS

PATRICK ANDERSON
pages 17, 18, 22.

CARLO BORLENGHI
page vi.

DAVID BRANIGAN
pages v, vi, 6, 16, 30, 31, 41, 44, 49, 52, 61, 63, 68, 69, 70, 71, 72, 76, 77, 90, 91, 94, 95, 97, 98, 102, 103, 104, 107, 108, 109, 126, 127, 142, 144, 147.

ROBIN BRITTEN
page 31.

HECTOR ETCHEBASTER
page 16.

ALEXANDRE HADAD
page 143.

OSKAR KIHLBORG
pages iii, 2, 5, 6, 10, 12, 13, 14, 16, 17, 19, 20, 22, 24, 27, 28, 29, 32, 34, 35, 36, 42, 45, 46, 48, 51, 52, 53, 54, 55, 59, 64, 65, 66, 72, 73, 74, 75, 76, 77, 78, 79, 80, 81, 83, 84, 86, 87, 88, 89, 90, 92, 93, 94, 95, 96, 98, 100, 101, 105, 106, 108, 136, 138, 140, 141, 142, 143, 144, 145, 147, 148.

MARÍA MUIÑA
pages 16, 26, 47.

JON NASH
pages ii, 9, 31, 87, 88, 89.

MARTIN STOCKBRIDGE
pages 13, 40, 80.

PAUL TODD
pages 11, 91, 143.

RICK TOMLINSON
pages iii, 5, 16, 17, 22, 152.

Photo Credits

Acknowledgments

My greatest thanks must go to the participants in the Volvo Ocean Race 2005–06. Without their commitment to sending vital news and information back from the race course, and to taking time out for onshore interviews, this story of what life is like when you are living at the extreme edge of adventure could never be told.

Thanks too to the other contributors. Personal insights into past races, and views from the inside for many aspects of this race, have greatly enhanced the content.

From my own side, this book could not have been created to such a tight deadline without a considerable amount of dedicated assistance from many others, in particular my personal assistant, Liz Christmas. This project was her induction into the world of book writing and serious deadlines, and she passed the test in the most consummate, professional manner.

To my media mates—Guy Swindells, Cameron Kelleher, Riath Al-Samarrai, Amanda Blackley, and Rachel Morgan—who made 8 months of travelling the world with this race that much more pleasurable, and who were always there to help with information and interviews, a big "thank you." Likewise, Oskar Kihlborg, Jon Nash, and Dave Branigan, whose superb photographs have brought a magnificent visual perspective to *Life at the Extreme.*

The efforts of Lizzie Green in the Volvo Ocean Race office must also be recognised. She was the captain of the ship for this project from start to finish and did everything possible to make my task easier. The same must be said of the publishers, Alex and Susan Kahan, and their team at Nomad Press. Professionals all.

My thanks also go to the Volvo Ocean Race CEO, Glenn Bourke, and Volvo Ocean Race commercial director, Anders Lofgren, for presenting me with the opportunity to deliver this story.

And finally, thanks to a true legend of racing around the planet, Grant Dalton, for taking the time to write the foreword.

Rob Mundle